The Art of Overcoming

The Art of Overcoming

Letting God Turn Your Endings into Beginnings

Tim Timberlake

with Justin Jaquith

W PUBLISHING GROUP

AN IMPRINT OF THOMAS NELSON

Published in Nashville, Tennessee, by W Publishing, an imprint of Thomas Nelson.

The author is represented by The Bindery Agency.

Thomas Nelson titles may be purchased in bulk for educational, business, fundraising, or sales promotional use. For information, please email SpecialMarkets@ThomasNelson.com.

ISBN 978-0-7852-3897-3 (audiobook)
ISBN 978-0-7852-3896-6 (eBook)
ISBN 978-0-7852-3895-9 (TP)

Library of Congress Control Number: 2022944347

Printed in the United States of America

23 24 25 26 27 LBC 5 4 3 2 1

To my son, Max. Your name was almost Rocket (true story). May you soar above any circumstance or challenge that life brings your way. I love you!

Contents

Contents

PART III – EULOGY: COMMEMORATION

PART IV – RECESSIONAL: CLOSURE

INTRODUCTION

Football, Faith, and Moving Forward

I love football. When I tell people that, I usually get one of two responses. Either they enthusiastically agree and start talking about "their" team or the latest Super Bowl predictions—or they sigh and admit, "I've never understood the rules of football. It's so confusing."

Here's the thing, though: *none* of us understands the rules of football. At least not all of them. Even the commentators get confused by the referees' calls sometimes, and they have to call up an expert, who makes an educated guess about what just happened. It's hilarious. Half the fun of football is trying to decipher what is going on. The point is not to have the game totally figured out but rather to watch your team overcome the opposition through strategy, skill, and grit. And, of course, to eat ridiculous quantities of junk food while doing so.

One more thing. Football, like any sport, is at its best when the underdog comes from behind against unbelievable odds and wins the game. You've probably seen games like this: with mere minutes remaining, the coaches and players find a way to overcome impossible circumstances. Meanwhile, everyone watching is screaming their lungs out and spilling the aforementioned junk food on the floor.

Life is a lot like football in at least two ways. First, *it's confusing*. We spend a great deal of time trying to understand what just happened, what is happening now, and what needs to happen next. In life, though, we are not fans stretched out across a couch, eating carbs and yelling at a screen; rather, we are active participants on the field, fighting to overcome what can feel like wave after wave of resistance.

The goal of human existence is not to have everything figured out, though. The goal is to *live*. As in, to breathe. To exist. To be fully alive. Not just to survive but to *be* and to *do* and to *become* all God has in mind for us. That includes things like loving people around us, knowing God better, fulfilling our potential, walking in our calling, growing in our character, and many other messy, chaotic, nonlinear things. We won't always know what's going on, and that's okay.

> **The goal of human existence is not to have everything figured out, though. The goal is to *live*.**

The second way life is like football is that *it's hard*. It is full of setbacks, losses, disappointments, pain, and tragedy. I'm not being pessimistic here—I'm being real. Most of us, most of the time, feel like the underdogs. However, our enemy is not an eleven-player team of human wrecking balls waiting for us to hike the football; rather, we are up against a lineup of difficult situations that aren't waiting for anything. They are already pushing and shoving their way into our lives.

I'm not just talking about the "normal" challenges of life either. I'm talking about the unforeseen ones. The blows. The losses. The unexpected setbacks. The ones that make us feel like we're losing at life. How do we process these moments? Do we panic in the face of pain? Or do we show up and *play*?

The Art of Overcoming is primarily about dealing with loss, grief, and hurt. It's about refusing to allow the things that look like endings to discourage or derail you, and instead, letting God turn them into beginnings. When life is confusing and difficult, don't give up. Show up. Step up. Level up. And *look* up. You're not doing this all on your own. No matter what difficult moment or painful loss you're facing, God is with you.

Let me warn you, though, that the "art of overcoming" sounds a lot more romantic than the actual *process* of overcoming. Most of overcoming is simply not quitting. Like football, it's a messy combination of strategy, skill, and grit that carries you through the confusion and the pain until you emerge triumphant on the other side. Overcoming is not about understanding everything or living without any pain but about finding ways to process in a healthy way the strange, scary, and sometimes devastating circumstances you go through. It's about coming out better on the other side, which probably won't happen the same way twice.

That's why it's an art.

Death Is Never the End

I'm going to use a rather unusual metaphor throughout this book: a funeral. Why would I do that? Death is even more confusing than football after all. And more painful. More complex. More final.

That's exactly my point. When life throws tragedies and losses our way, those things don't just make us feel like we're a few points behind in a game. They feel more like death. And they are like death, in a sense. I call them "little deaths" or "death experiences," and they have more power to perplex or paralyze us than we might realize. I originally thought about titling this book *The Funeral*, but my publisher talked me out of that idea, fortunately. However, I'd still like to use the structure of a typical southern funeral to explore how we can process a wide range of loss, pain, disappointment, and grief.

Why use such a dramatic metaphor? Because loss deserves recognition, pain needs space to be felt, disappointment requires time to process, and grief demands attention. Too often we try to gloss over the difficult things we face, as if by ignoring them we could make them disappear. We understand the value of funerals when it comes to the death of a friend or family member, but often we forget (or don't know how) to properly grieve the day-to-day disappointments and losses that wound our souls.

We need to be intentional about honoring these little deaths. That is what a funeral does: it honors loss. It forces us to stop the hectic pace of life for a moment and acknowledge what is no longer present. Funerals are about recognizing absence, processing pain, celebrating the past—and moving toward the future. No, they aren't a lot of fun, but fun isn't the point. The point is honesty and healing and hope.

We all need to grieve from time to time because none of us is immune to pain and loss. We've all experienced disappointment, hurt, tragedy, sorrow, fear, and grief. Anything that creates a profound sense of pain or loss is a form of death, and these things can feel nearly as final as literal death.

Maybe a loved one passed away unexpectedly. Perhaps a start-up business we poured our heart and our savings into went under. Or a best friend betrayed us. An employer fired us. A family member abused us. A medical diagnosis upended our life. A child is struggling with mental illness. Our "perfect" marriage disintegrated in front of our eyes. An addiction has broken us inside and out. A parent or sibling cut us out of their life. We had to sell our dream house.

A business partnership soured and we lost our investment and our dreams for the future.

These moments feel terrible. Sometimes they knock us to the floor. Often they seem insurmountable. We find ourselves angry, depressed, and confused because what we are experiencing is the last thing we expected. Where is God? How could he let this happen? What good is faith? How can there be a future after this?

Here's a point I'll return to again and again: Just as physical death is not the end but rather a beginning of new life in heaven with God, so our little deaths are not the end. We don't overcome by avoiding death; we overcome by walking through death. Therein lies the challenge. When we face death experiences, how should we respond?

> At some point the loss must be accepted and life must begin again.

This book attempts to address that question. Notice I didn't say *answer* that question, because grief doesn't have an answer. It can, however, be addressed. It can be acknowledged and respected. It can be listened to and empowered. And often, those are the first steps to healing.

The goal of this book, then, is to help you grieve, process, and eventually bury those things that represent death in your life. Not in a dismissive, gaslighting way, as if they didn't matter, but respectfully, gently, and in your own time and manner. To put it another way, don't skip the funeral, but also don't stand there staring at an open casket forever. At some point the loss must be accepted and life must begin again.

I'm not a psychologist or a therapist, so I don't intend this to be a professional how-to manual about dealing with grief. Instead, I want to come alongside you and share what I've discovered through my own seasons of pain and loss, what I've learned as a pastor by walking with others through their death experiences, and what I see in the Bible. By the way, if your beliefs are different from mine, that's perfectly fine. I'm not going to force my faith on anyone or try to prove that I am right and someone else is wrong. Faith is a very personal journey, one everyone must take for themselves. I recognize the limitations and subjectivity I bring to the table. No book could fully address subjects as complex and personal as loss, pain, and grief. That's why I hope you come away from these pages not just with information but with the motivation and faith you need to work through your own process of grief.

Ultimately, no one can grieve for you, and no one can tell you how to grieve. We can grieve *with* you, though. Consider this book an attempt to do that. In the following chapters, I won't shy away from the reality of pain, but I won't give in to it either. Instead, I will explore what it means to walk through suffering and come out stronger on the other side. Rather than seeking a cheap, fake hope that pretends loss isn't real or doesn't matter, we must pursue an honest, eyes-open, real-life hope rooted in a God who brings good from evil, light from dark, and life from death.

Death is not the end, although in the moment it often feels like it is. Rather, it is a season to reflect, to honor, and to grow. It is the end of one chapter but the beginning of a new one. The new doesn't diminish the old, and looking toward the future doesn't mean we forget the past. Instead, we must learn to hold loss and hope at the same time.

That's what a funeral is all about.

How This Book Is Organized

I use the imagery of a traditional funeral ceremony as a framework to look at the "death experiences" we face in the unpredictable journey of life. These experiences include all the grief, disappointment, tragedy, loss, pain, suffering, abuse, and sorrow that come our way. By the way, I'll use all those terms somewhat interchangeably throughout the book. They aren't really synonyms, of course, but they do point to different facets of these death experiences.

Part I: A Matter of Life and Death. The opening section is about *contradiction*. How do life and death coexist? What about victories and losses? Promotions and setbacks? What role does faith play in it all? Can we find joy in sorrow or hope in pain? We will explore several foundational perspectives on grief and failure and disappointments that set the course for the rest of the book.

Part II: Processional. We then move on to *confrontation*, where we face head-on the reality of our death experiences. We take an honest look at how to grieve the losses we face in six areas of life: people, dreams, security, control, sin, and certainty.

Part III: Eulogy. Here we focus on *commemoration*. We look at how to memorialize and honor what has been lost and how to process our feelings in a healthy way. In these chapters, we explore ways to have a healthy perspective on the pain we are experiencing, including the topics of nuance, pain, emotions, timing, resilience, and forgiveness.

Part IV: Recessional. The final section is about *closure*, about moving forward after death or loss. We can remember what has died—whether good or bad—as we transition to a new beginning and face the future with faith. We'll explore peace, gratitude, hope, growth, joy, and acceptance.

It's likely that you are reading this book because you or someone close to you is going through a difficult time. Whether that difficulty is best described as loss, disappointment, pain, grief, or something else, please know that I am praying for you as I write this book. I believe God has a purpose in the pain. His grace is always strongest when we are weakest, and no matter what you might be facing, you can find strength in him. My prayer is that the principles and stories in the following pages would help you process your pain and find God's healing.

Remember, it might look dark now, but this is not the end. As David wrote in Psalms, "Weeping may stay for the night, but rejoicing comes in the morning" (30:5). No matter what your past holds, I believe you can have a full, joyful, fulfilling future.

That future might not include watching football while eating junk food and yelling at a screen. That's fine. I've learned not to try talking anyone else into loving football. But I do think your future includes loving *life*, even when that life has its share of death. After all, if death reminds us of anything, it's that life must be lived to the fullest, and death cannot win because we were created to overcome.

I think we can all agree on that.

PART I

A Matter of Life and Death

Contradiction

In order to let God turn an ending into a beginning, we have to acknowledge that the ending has happened. That seems like it should go without saying, but letting go is hard to do. It's painful to process the death of a dream, a relationship, a career, or a goal we've worked hard to achieve. It feels like a contradiction to our faith, so we usually fight it as hard as we can, trying to avoid (or even deny) the pain or loss or hurt that has come upon us.

Death never makes sense, and loss always creates complicated questions. How do we go on living once something or someone we loved has died? What role does faith play in loss? Can we find joy in sorrow, peace in pain, hope in suffering? And where is God in the middle of all this?

It is in the contradictions of death and loss that God often makes himself known most clearly. That is what faith in God means: to hold fast to what we believe about the God we know, even when circumstances are shifting and crumbling around us. As we look at the intersection of faith and loss in the coming chapters, we will discover that they are not contradictory at all. In fact, they work together.

ONE

Butter Beans and Fried Chicken

Nobody does death quite like the South.

That might sound a bit dark, but it's a good thing. In the South we take time to celebrate a loved one's life. We process our grief together, out loud and in public. Funerals for us are not an event to be endured or a topic to be avoided; they are an experience to be shared. They are a ritual, a tradition, an event. The deceased might be your wife's coworker's spouse's father, whom you met one time at a party fourteen years ago, but you do whatever it takes to be at his funeral because that's just how we do it here. I know other countries have their own ways of honoring the memory of loved ones who have passed on, and every region of the United States does too. As for me, I find comfort and peace in the unhurried, time-honored funeral rituals of the South.

As a pastor I've been to hundreds of funerals over the years, and the term conjures up a mix of strong memories and emotions. There is grief, of course, and anger, and pain, and loss. But there is also peace, hope, and joy, because heaven is never more real to us than

3

when we're in the presence of death. Funerals also make me think of friends, of family, of embraces, and—to be honest—of really good food. southern funerals are not complete without a reception where some good ole soul food waits in all its culinary glory. Think butter beans, fried chicken, corn on the cob, apple pie—funeral meals are definitely "comfort food."

Welcome to Funerals in the South

A typical southern funeral begins with the processional at the church. The preacher leads the way down the aisle to the front, followed by the pallbearers carrying the casket, and then the family members, who are seated on the front row. At this point the congregation might sing a classic gospel hymn or a song that was special to the deceased.

Next the minister gives the eulogy. He describes the life of the deceased: their story, their accomplishments, their family. Oftentimes a few stories are shared about the person's quirks and idiosyncrasies, played for laughs, and maybe even some delicate references to mistakes they made or challenges they struggled to overcome. After another song and maybe some comments from friends and family, the service ends.

Then comes the recessional. The casket is carried out to a waiting hearse, followed by the family. Everyone loads up in their vehicles and forms a long line of cars. Then they drive slowly, headlights on, hazard lights blinking, sometimes led by a police cruiser, until they reach the cemetery, where the group holds a short graveside ceremony.

That's not the true end of the funeral, though—from there, people head over to the reception. Grief has a way of making you hungry. But not just for butter beans and fried chicken. It makes you hungry for conversations with friends, for reconnecting with family members who came from out of town, for long talks about deep issues, for comforting hugs, for laughter and joy.

This reception can last for hours, and I think it is the most fulfilling, comforting, healing part of the whole process. People trade stories about the departed, ranging from hilarious to sentimental to unbelievable. The mood swings back and forth between tears and laughter, grief and gratitude, loss and acceptance, as people close a chapter on the past and begin to contemplate life without their loved one.

That is a funeral in the South. It's a celebration of life, a recognition of death, and a ceremony to help process the transition, surrounded by family and friends.

I'm not saying funerals are easy; they are not. Death is an enemy, the Bible says, and anyone who has lost a close family member or friend understands how foreign death feels to the human experience. The gaping hole left by death is unique among all kinds of pain. It can be heartrending, life-altering, traumatic. No matter what region or country we come from, we are all familiar with the sting of death. It is something that connects the human experience around the world.

This, after all, is why funerals exist, isn't it? Not so much for the dead and departed but for the living who remain. Funerals help us process death. They give us closure. They are a chance to celebrate the gift of life, acknowledge the reality of loss, and begin our healing journeys. Funerals are not empty rituals or traditions but a necessary, healthy step in the process of laying the past to rest and moving into the future.

Funerals are necessary not just because death is inevitable but because life is beautiful. They are a way to memorialize, process, celebrate, and bid goodbye. They mark the end of one life, yes; but they also recognize that the rest of us must now adjust and move forward without the presence of a beloved friend or family member. That's what people mean when they comment after the service, "That was such a beautiful funeral." They are saying that the ceremony was a fitting celebration of a life well lived. Yes, they are still sad—but a life was given the honor it was due.

Take Time to Grieve

In the same way, the smaller "death experiences" that we face in life deserve to be recognized, which unfortunately is something we often forget. A business fails and we rush on to start a new one. A dream comes crashing down, and we pretend we didn't care that much in the first place. A significant other breaks up with us, so we scrub them from our Instagram feeds and try to convince ourselves we knew it wouldn't last anyway.

Why are we in such a hurry to move on from the past? We need to take time to grieve our losses. I know it hurts to think about them, but they were a valuable, influential part of our lives, and that means they were important. Why? Because *we* are important. If we minimize or dismiss our pain too quickly, it's as if we are minimizing or dismissing ourselves.

Remember, in the eyes of God (and probably a lot of people in your life), you are infinitely valuable. That means your dreams are valuable. So are your feelings. And your plans. Your relationships. Your business ventures. Your children. Your house. Your pets. And anything else you care about. Losing any of those things will naturally cause grief, and that grief is valid and justified because of *who you are*, not because of the size or nature of what was lost. Don't let anyone else tell you that your loss doesn't matter, and don't tell yourself that either.

Of course, this can be taken to an extreme. We've all known people (or maybe we've been these people) who can't get over a loss. I can't help but wonder if our inability to deal with loss is sometimes connected to our unwillingness to properly grieve it in the first place. It's hard to heal from something we deny ever happened. Some of us need to tone down the toxic positivity and allow ourselves the luxury of brutal honesty.

Yes, that honesty hurts. It hurts like a funeral. But it also *heals* like a funeral. When we're finally able to lay to rest the loss, the pain, the betrayal, the abandonment—that's when we begin to find *our* rest.

That letting go, that hurting-to-healing cycle, is something we have to learn. Understanding what to let go (as well as when and how to let it go) is an often-overlooked part of the art of overcoming. We tend to assume that to overcome, we need to conquer everything in our path. We must get our way and reach our goals no matter what. But nobody can do that, at least not all the time. We are human beings, which means we are finite and fallible. We overcome not by imposing our will wherever we go but by learning to give and take, end and start, grieve and rejoice, according to what is required in the moment.

Overcoming often looks like losing, at least at first. If that seems backward, think about these words of Jesus: "For whoever wants to save their life will lose it, but whoever loses their life for me will find it" (Matthew 16:25). Jesus was talking about following him, about being willing to sacrifice certain pursuits, privileges, or pleasures in order to obey him fully. The principle goes beyond just spirituality, though. It points to an approach to life that isn't afraid of death. It's a willingness to let go of what is good to gain what is best.

How to Overcome by Letting Go

Letting go is easier said than done. Change is never easy. Change— even good change—always means the loss of something. Often we focus on the losses of the past because it hurts, and pain has a way of stealing our focus and holding our attention. It takes foresight and maturity to look beyond the present pain and realize something better is coming. In loss, pain, and death, let's not forget the blessings ahead.

Many heroes of the Bible had to say goodbye to things they cared for deeply. We remember the victory at the end of their stories, but we often forget the emotional choices they made along the way to let go of a past or a dream or a relationship that needed to be laid to rest. Only then could they step into the future God was offering them.

Remember in Genesis 22 when God asked Abraham to give up his son? Isaac was his only son, his promised son, his beloved son, the answer to decades of prayer and patience. God's instruction must have felt like death to Abraham. But he was willing to let go, and God applauded him for his faith and trust. In fact, the Bible calls him "the father of all who believe" (Romans 4:11).

Or how about when Moses tried and failed to deliver the Israelites in his own strength, then fled to hide in the wilderness in fear and shame (Exodus 2)? I can only imagine the guilt and insecurity that must have plagued him for decades. Then one day, God told him to go back to the land of Egypt. Moses had more excuses than a teenager being told to clean his room, but God finally talked him into it. Moses had to let two things die: his idea of how Israel would be set free (control) and his feelings of failure (shame). When he let go of those, God used him to deliver Israel from Egypt.

Consider Ruth as well. Remember how much she lost? Her husband, father-in-law, and brother-in-law, to start with. But that didn't stop her. In pursuit of a better future, she was brave enough to give up a lot more, including her homeland and her own family. She followed her mother-in-law, Naomi, to Israel, where she found love, family, and prosperity. Her story had the kind of ending that fairy tales are made of. We'll look at her life in more detail in a later chapter.

Joseph had to die to his ambitions and dreams when his brothers sold him into slavery in Egypt. Hannah had to leave her son Samuel behind to grow up at the temple. David had to say goodbye to his best friend, Jonathan. Esther had to leave her adoptive uncle to move into the palace of a maniacal, pagan ruler. Nehemiah had to leave a king's palace and risk everything to rebuild Jerusalem. Jesus had to find comfort and healing after his cousin John the Baptist was killed. Mary had to say goodbye to her son on the cross. I could go on and on, but you get the picture. Overcoming is not just about what we *get*; it's about what we *give up*.

These stories from the heroes of our faith should remind us that letting go is just as much a part of faith as holding on. We need to remove the stigma that is often attached to grief. What are we so embarrassed about? What are we so afraid of? Closing a business, going bankrupt, or having a chronic illness doesn't mean we are failures. Nor does it mean that we don't have faith. These circumstances and others like them simply mean we are alive, and we are human, and we are normal, and we are *moving forward*.

There is a natural movement or trajectory to life, and what works for one season doesn't necessarily work for the next. Losing, leaving, and laying to rest are necessary stages of growth. Nobody likes to lose, but if we can't lose, we can't gain either. We will just stay where we are, and that's unnatural.

For example, my son is at the young age where he seems to change every day. That's a good thing, of course, because it means he is developing new talents and skills. But it also means he is leaving behind some things that my wife and I love and will miss. Right now, for example, he says "expecting of" when he means "speaking of." We drove past an airport recently and he said, "Expecting of airplanes . . ." We're going to miss that little quirk and so much more as he grows older. The way he climbs into our laps. His childlike passion and innocence. His physical nearness all the time. His laughter. His dependence and trust. His incessant questions (okay, we might not miss those). Growth is bittersweet, but the opposite—staying the same—is not healthy or natural.

We need to reframe "overcoming" in a more realistic way. It's not all rose petals and glitter. It's not all trophies and medals and awards. A lot of overcoming is simply moving forward, growing, and adapting as we go. It is leaving the past behind without bitterness or regret, but rather with honor, knowing what we had was important for a season, but that the season has ended. In other words, we learn to let things rest in peace without losing our peace.

> **We learn to let things rest in peace without losing our peace.**

How about you? Are you facing any little deaths right now? Are you finding it difficult to let something go, leave something behind, or lay something to rest? If so, it means you're alive and normal. Don't feel bad for feeling bad. That will only make things worse. Instead, lean into your grief. Explore it, feel it, honor it, learn from it.

Remember, this is a process. It's a cycle. If you don't walk through the steps of honoring your loss, grieving it, burying it, and returning to life, then your little deaths can become so much more than they ever should have been. Disappointment and pain that are not dealt with turn into guilt, shame, anger, bitterness, fear. Death takes on a life of its own, and it begins to choke out the real life, the abundant life, that God desires to give you.

We'll talk a lot more about the process of dealing with grief and loss in the following pages, but for now, just know that better days are ahead. I truly believe that. You don't need to be in a hurry to get there, though. Take the time to bury what needs to be buried and let God heal your heart. In due time you'll find yourself enjoying metaphorical butter beans, rolls, fried chicken, and apple pie as you pay your respects to the past and become excited for the future.

TWO

Endings Are Beginnings

I experienced death and sorrow firsthand when my father passed away from cancer. I was only eighteen years old at the time, and I didn't really know how to process what was happening. Even though he had been terminally ill, I wasn't prepared to lose him. He was my dad, after all, forever tall and full of faith. I always assumed there would be more chances to talk with him, to learn from him, to find strength in him. He would always be there for me.

Until he wasn't.

Death took him too soon, and we were left to piece together a fatherless reality that didn't make sense. And so we did. Because that's what the living do after they come face-to-face with death. They just keep living. They cling to life, and they find new life out of death.

I'd be lying if I said the process was easy. I hated God more often than I loved him during those first few months. I resented him more often than I trusted him. But over time I worked through my grief and anger. I came to know God in a more real, humble, raw way. I realized he wasn't frustrated by my doubt or grief. Quite the opposite: he wanted me to draw close to him and process what I was feeling in the safety of his arms. Impossible as it seemed at first, I came to trust him again. More than ever, in fact.

Today death has less power to shake my soul because I've already walked through the pain it has to offer. God brought me out on the other side, and I'm a better, bigger person because of it.

It goes without saying, but my dad is in a much better place too. His last months included a lot of pain, and heaven brought relief to suffering. Today and forever after he's enjoying the peace and presence of the God he loved so much and served so faithfully.

Did we suffer a lot because of his death? Yes. Do I miss him? Of course. Do I wish he were still here? Absolutely. But his death was not the end of all things good. It didn't rob us of happiness and security and joy forever. It didn't destroy our family or our faith.

Why? Because God was, is, and always will be faithful to bring life out of death. He did it for my father by taking him to heaven. He did it for my family by being a Father to the fatherless. He did it for me by leading me into a deeper relationship with him.

Death led to new life, as death always does.

Death Has Lost Its Sting

If you, like me, have ever had to deal with the sudden loss of a friend or family member, you know the terrible power of death when it strikes. It's the sucker punch that drops us in our tracks, the blow that leaves us feeling powerless, hopeless, defeated. Nothing can stop it, and once it happens, nothing can reverse it. All that is left is for those who remain to grieve the loss, pick up the pieces, and try to carry on. There is no going back to how things were, only stumbling forward into an uncertain future.

Death is the end.

Or is it?

You see, the sting of death—whether we are talking about literal death or simply the loss of something we valued—is found in its finality. That's why people are so afraid of it. That's why it hurts so much to lose someone close to us or something important to us. We can never get back what we've lost, and that creates grief.

But what if death is not as final as we think? What if death has less power, less authority, less of a grasp on the human soul than our experiences would lead us to believe? Again, I'm not talking just about physical death but about our death experiences in general. What if loss and grief aren't as final as they feel in the moment?

> ## We can never get back what we've lost, and that creates grief.

The more I read the Bible and the longer I follow Jesus, the more I've seen these simple truths at work: What we think are endings are usually just beginnings. What we think is loss often turns out to be gain (Philippians 1:21). What should be weakness somehow becomes strength (2 Corinthians 12:9). What was meant for evil results in good (Genesis 50:20). Why? Because that's how powerful and good God is. He has a way of turning the worst thing that could happen into the best thing that could happen.

Nowhere is this clearer than in the promise of heaven. When it comes to the human soul, the hope of life after death lies at the core of the gospel message. The death of the body seems insurmountable, but God promises us that someday, death itself will be defeated. Death is temporary; heaven is eternal. This is a core tenet of the Christian faith. It's the reason funerals so often point to God and heaven. It's why families who have lost a loved one comfort one another by saying that someday they will be together again.

If you consider yourself a Jesus follower, it's likely that you have a strong confidence in eternal life. Even if you aren't sure about God, Jesus, faith, or heaven, you probably hope there is more to the human existence than just the wonder and woes this planet offers us for the few decades we're here. There is probably an inkling inside you that death is not the end; a twinge in the back of your consciousness that points somewhere outside of space and time. For me, I believe the collection of writings we call the Bible provides a divine glimpse of the other side of that veil, and I find great encouragement in its pages. God's promise is not just life until death but life *in* death, *through* death, and *after* death.

For example, Isaiah wrote, "[God] will swallow up death forever. The Sovereign LORD will wipe away the tears from all faces" (Isaiah 25:8).

Hosea spoke for God when he said, "I will deliver this people from the power of the grave; I will redeem them from death. Where, O death, are your plagues? Where, O grave, is your destruction?" (Hosea 13:14).

The apostle Paul quoted from both of those ancient prophets and then added, "The sting of death is sin, and the power of sin is the law. But thanks be to God! He gives us the victory through our Lord Jesus Christ" (1 Corinthians 15:56–57).

The grave doesn't get the last word. God does. One day death will be swallowed up in the victory of heaven. This is called the *resurrection*, and it's when those who have died become alive again. Death is defeated once and for all, and life wins in the end.

This raises two important questions: What earthly good is a heavenly resurrection? What does the promise of heaven have to do with the challenges and tragedies we face on earth? You might be thinking, *Heaven sounds great, but I'm not planning on going there anytime soon. Right now I'm more worried about my shrinking bank account and my nonexistent dating life. I want to know how to deal with the disappointment and grief that threaten to overwhelm me today. Heaven will have to wait.*

Those are valid points. Heaven is not as far off as it sounds, though. As a matter of fact, in many ways the kingdom of heaven is present and active on earth today. Following are a few ways the resurrection life of heaven can help us deal with our death experiences on earth.

1. If God can defeat physical death, he can defeat any death.

   The lesson of the resurrection is that nothing is too hard for God. If physical death can't stop him, then our little deaths certainly can't either. That should boost our faith and encourage us to pray and trust no matter how bleak the outlook is. Nothing is too hard for God.

2. The same power that will raise us from the dead is at work in us now.

   In other words, the resurrection power of heaven starts on earth. The apostle Paul wrote, "And if the Spirit of him who raised Jesus from the dead is living in you, he who raised Christ from the dead will also give life to your mortal bodies because of his Spirit who lives in you" (Romans 8:11). In this part of his letter, Paul was talking about God's grace to overcome the power and the effects of sin. The apostle didn't promise us immediate, absolute freedom from all pain and suffering, but he did tell us that God's power is actively at work *within us* even when the world *around us* is a mess. We might be facing a great deal of death, but God's life is always at work in us.

3. Just as physical death is a doorway to heaven, so our little deaths are often doorways into a better future.

As I pointed out earlier, endings are beginnings. They might feel like walls blocking the path, but eventually they turn out to be doorways into the future and the beginning of something far *better* than what we left behind. That doesn't diminish the value of what we lost, but it does remind us to keep our eyes and hearts open for greater blessings ahead.

These three observations won't take away the pain of loss, of course. The promise of heaven doesn't mean we won't feel any sorrow on earth. But it does mean sorrow is not the end. Death is leading us toward life. That means we can grieve what has passed away while also allowing faith to rise in our hearts for something better to come.

Life Always Comes Out of Death

Accepting that something better is coming can be hard to do because we don't know the future. All we know is the present—and we probably aren't too excited that it's suddenly changing. Transition is scary, even when what lies ahead is better than what we are leaving behind.

Have you ever imagined what must go through a baby's head when they are being born? I was present at the birth of our son, so I have a good idea what my wife was thinking by the end—that she was probably going to die, but she was going to kill me first. I can't even imagine what our son must have been thinking. He didn't ask to be born, and I'm sure he didn't enjoy the process one bit. He most likely would have chosen to stay in the womb, if anybody had asked him, even though he was so crammed in there that he couldn't move. He couldn't have imagined the freedom of the outside world, though. He didn't even have the language for it.

Sometimes I think death must be a little bit like that. We hold on so tightly to this world because we don't know what's next. I suspect that when we do get to heaven, we're going to wonder why we were so scared to die. The difference between heaven and earth is probably comparable to the difference between being inside the womb and outside the womb. But many of us fear death because we're afraid of what we don't know.

> **Little deaths terrify us because we can't visualize what's ahead.**

In the same way, out of fear of the unknown we often hold on to the people, places, or dreams that we are starting to lose. Little deaths terrify us because we can't visualize what's ahead. We don't have the language for it. We've never lived it. Therefore it's difficult for us to transition into the new world on the other side of the doorway.

I'm reminded of something Jesus told his disciples: "Very truly I tell you, unless a kernel of wheat falls to the ground and dies, it remains only a single seed. But if it dies, it produces many seeds" (John 12:24). Though he was talking about how his death would bring life to many, the principle can also be applied to other forms of dying.

Our little deaths are often like seeds: when something is buried, something greater springs forth. Maybe you were fired from a job that you didn't think you could live without. Now, five years later, you've built an entirely new career that you love and that is providing twice the income. Maybe you moved to a new city and found yourself alone and homesick, missing your past life. Then, after being vulnerable for a while and opening yourself up to new relationships, you made lifelong friends who you wouldn't trade for the world. Maybe you ended a toxic dating relationship after years of trying to make it work. Then, after the pain subsided, you met someone else, someone who truly valued you, and you found love, marriage, and a family.

Death is not the end. It's *an ending*, yes, but it's not *the end*. It's also a beginning, a necessary step before what is new can come into existence. Instead of panicking out of fear of the unknown, take a deep breath, choose to trust God, and walk through the doorway. That is your role and responsibility in the death process. If a shattered dream, lost job, broken relationship, or something else has left you reeling, it's up to you to process that death in the right way—and then move forward into newness.

Give whatever it is a proper funeral. Honor it, grieve it, process it. Then bury it in the ground of faith and return to the land of the living. Death is an event, not eternal limbo. It's a moment in time, or maybe a season—but it's not forever. Sooner or later what has passed away has to be left in the past.

If we can see our death experiences from God's eyes, we'll realize that death never wins. Again and again, it is swallowed up in sweet victory. Again and again, God gets the last word. Again and again, life triumphs over death.

And again and again, endings become beginnings.

THREE

Faith in the Dark

One Christmas when I was maybe six years old, I had two very specific requests. I wanted a particular kind of bicycle (which happened to be an expensive one, of course), and I wanted a Sega Genesis, the newest, hottest game console on the market. The problem was that my parents were on a tight budget. I didn't exactly know what a budget was, but I knew it meant they probably were not going to buy anything expensive.

So I decided to pull out the secret weapon: faith. I knew what faith was. Or at least I thought I did. I had heard my parents talk about "believing God" for things we needed and wanted as a family. By faith I understood that I had to pray, believe, and expect that Santa Claus would bring me what I wanted. I'm still not sure how Santa Claus made it into my theology, but kids' brains aren't exactly logical.

Anyway, I put my faith to work. I wrote down on a sheet of paper what I wanted Santa to bring me for Christmas. I prayed, I hoped, I believed, I declared, I confessed—I did all the things I knew how to do to make my faith work. God and Santa Claus were not going to get out of this one easily.

When Christmas rolled around, I didn't get the bike or the Sega

Genesis. I felt rather defeated, of course. I knew my parents were doing the best they could, so I didn't blame them. But I wondered what good having faith was if it couldn't even get the two main powers of the universe—God and Santa—to spring for a bike and a gaming console.

My dad noticed my dejection, and he asked me what was wrong. I said, "My faith didn't work."

He replied, "What do you mean your 'faith didn't work?' How do you know?"

"Well, I don't think my faith worked because I didn't get what I wanted."

Then my dad wisely explained to me that faith doesn't work the way I thought. We might not get what we *want*, but God makes sure we get what we *need*. Faith isn't about getting God to fulfill our every request or desire; it's about trusting that he knows what is best for us and will always take care of us. My dad told me that God cares about our desires and our dreams, and he often does give us things we want and ask for. But he doesn't have to. He is God, and he makes the best decision possible, which means we can always trust him.

I've had a few decades to practice my faith since then, and my dad was right. We don't always get what we wish for or even what we think we need. But God always knows best, and he always comes through. Faith isn't about twisting God's arm; it's about resting in his arms. It's about leaning on him and listening to him, especially when life doesn't make sense.

That's why faith is so important in our death experiences. In seasons of hurt, loss, and disappointment, we might not have what we want or wish for, but we can trust that we have what we need. Life isn't over, hope isn't lost, and God is still on the throne.

Even in death, we can find life.

Even in pain, we can make plans.

Even in the bad, we can expect good.

Even in loss, we can hold on to hope.

Death and faith go together. They are not mutually exclusive. Yet this is contrary to the way we often view faith. We seem to assume that going through a death experience must mean we lack faith. *If I just had more faith*, we think, *that sickness would be healed. That money would come in. That addiction would stop tormenting me.*

As my dad taught me, that's the wrong way to think about faith. And it's the wrong way to think about death. I would argue that death experiences can be the greatest proof of your

> **Faith in God shines brightest in dark moments.**

faith. Faith in God shines brightest in dark moments. That's exactly why it exists—to provide strength when nothing makes sense.

They Died in Faith

Allowing faith to coexist with death is important because sometimes we try to use faith to *avoid* death when God is asking us to use faith to *deal with* death. Instead of walking through death experiences with grace, we think we can believe, hope, trust, claim, quote, and pray our way out of them. When that doesn't work, we blame ourselves for our lack of faith, or we get mad at God for not holding up his end of the deal, or we pendulum swing back and forth between the two.

I was raised in an environment of faith. I've heard about faith my whole life. I've seen faith used and abused. I've seen it help people and I've seen it condemn people. I've preached about it, practiced it, wrestled with it, got mad at it, been confused by it, relied upon it, and been carried by it.

Blaming pain, loss, or any death experience on not having enough faith puts way too much pressure on people. Death, by definition, is beyond human control. If you think every bad thing that happens is because you didn't have enough faith, you're going to spend a lot of time feeling ashamed and condemned. Plus, what we are suffering or what we have lost is only part of our story. Faith in God allows us to see our little deaths in their wider context: they are just one part of a complex, long, layered, beautiful life.

Hebrews 11 lists numerous people from Israel's history. For each one it says, "By faith so-and-so did such-and-such." It's easy to look at that list and think, *Wow, those men and women were incredible. They believed, and God did miracles. Their faith was proved by their lives.*

But look at verse 13: "All these people were still living by faith when they died. They did not receive the things promised; they only saw them and welcomed them from a distance, admitting that they were foreigners and strangers on earth."

Did you catch that? They didn't just live in faith; they died in faith. They proved their faith not just by the way they lived but also by the way they died—in faith, knowing that God is faithful in this age and in the age to come.

What if we stopped looking at our death experiences as a sign that we *lacked* faith and instead looked at them as simply another way to *walk by* faith? What if we stopped thinking we somehow *failed* God and instead remembered we are *following* God? That would change our whole perspective on loss, pain, and disappointment. It would change our perspective on ourselves too. We would give ourselves space to grieve and time to heal instead of hiding our pain or beating ourselves up over it.

Having faith in God doesn't mean you never lose a job, a loved one, or a friendship. It means that even when you lose what you thought you couldn't survive without, you keep living. You keep loving. You keep giving. Your loss is real, but so is your faith. Your pain runs deep, but your faith runs deeper. Your circumstances have changed, but God hasn't.

If you are going through something difficult right now, you could be feeling challenged in your faith. It might be a struggle to get up in the morning, to continue trying, to keep believing. That struggle can make you think you are weak. You might even think you're letting God down because you're having such a difficult time believing that he'll take care of you.

I'd like to suggest that not only are you a hero for just showing up every day, but your faith is probably a lot stronger than you're giving yourself credit for. Why? Because you're still here. You're still moving forward. You're still trying to make sense of things.

That is faith.

Faith Grows Best Under Pressure

Just because your faith is stronger than you realize doesn't mean it can't continue to grow. That is one of the side benefits of going through hard times: our faith grows and deepens.

Early on in my walk with God, I often wondered why it seemed like other people had bigger faith than I did. They believed in God in such a deep, strong way. One day I came across a scripture saying that God gives each of us a measure of faith (Romans 12:3), which I understood to mean that faith is a gift from God. If other people's faith was so much stronger than mine, I wondered, had God simply given them a greater measure?

Sometime later I happened to be watching a show on the Discovery Channel, and it mentioned that every human body has the same number of muscles. That got me thinking. I have the same number of muscles as a bodybuilder. So what's the difference? Obviously the difference is how hard they work and how well they develop their muscles.

It's the same with our faith. How we work and develop our faith is what makes the difference. Often we think that our faith is weak or insufficient. The reality, however, is that our faith is there—it just needs to grow. God created us with the capacity to strengthen our faith.

How does that happen? By using our faith. By exercising it. By leaning on and listening to God until our ability to believe his promises grows stronger. In practical terms, that usually happens best in times of pressure, difficulty, loss, sorrow, and threat. Those are places where God is needed, and therefore those are the places where *faith* in God develops.

Now, if we're not careful, comparing faith to a muscle can send the wrong message. It can put too much emphasis on our effort and actions. Our faith should be in God, but sometimes we put our faith in our faith. We assume that if we believe and pray and hope hard enough, if we think better and do better and become better, then God won't let bad stuff happen. We trust our faith instead of trusting our God.

Faith can't point to us, though. That misses the whole point. It's not about beating down doors and punching out enemies. It's not about jumping over walls and conquering cities. At least not when we're attempting all that on our own. Faith is only and always about *God*. Faith points to his strength, his faithfulness, and his presence, not to our incredible power or cleverness.

Often faith in God is less about action and more about resting, letting go, and waiting. That's why it tends to develop during the little death seasons we go through. When nothing makes sense and we are powerless to change our circumstances, we turn to God. The moment that happens, we've activated our faith and begun to grow.

When you're going through dark times, one of the best ways to build your faith in God is by reading the Bible. The Word of God will increase your faith and courage. The examples of heroes of faith in its pages—both the ones who saw miracles come to pass and the ones who died in faith—will inspire you. Besides Scripture, things such as prayer and worship will build your faith and strength as well.

Challenges grow your faith, and greater faith will help you face future challenges better. It's an ongoing process of growth and improvement. You'll still go through pain and loss at times because death is a part of this world. But those things won't derail you. They'll only make you stronger.

Live Free from Fear

This understanding that faith and death often go together doesn't just help you face loss, pain, or disappointment with confidence. It also helps you live free from the *fear* of those things. That is, faith in God helps you view an uncertain future with confidence and peace, even though you are fully aware that difficult moments might be waiting around the corner.

A lot of people live in terror that "something bad" will happen. They are afraid of tragedy, failure, bankruptcy, divorce, getting fired, cancer, abandonment, rejection, and other adversities. These are the death experiences we've been talking about—except they haven't even happened yet. They are just hypotheticals. And yet because of fear, death has a grip on people's hearts and keeps them from fully enjoying the abundant life in front of them.

I remember hearing a story about a little boy who was afraid to sleep in his room by himself. Every night he would run into his parents' room and yell, "There's a monster under my bed! There's a monster under my bed!" The father would grab a flashlight, go into the boy's room, and show him that there was nothing under his bed. This happened night after night.

Finally the father had a great idea. While his son was at school, he sawed off the legs of the bed, making it flush with the ground. That evening, he showed the boy that the bed was touching the floor, and nothing could possibly fit under it. Everyone went to bed, and the parents were confident they would finally get a good night's sleep.

No such luck. A few minutes later, the boy came running in and screamed to his parents, "There's a monster under my bed!"

Obviously the problem wasn't the monsters under the bed but the monsters in his *head*. It didn't matter that the fear was illogical or that the bed was flat on the floor. He couldn't be convinced the monsters weren't real because they *were* real—to him. And that's all that mattered.

As we grow up, the monsters under the bed fade away. But the monsters in our heads often grow even stronger. We can end up living in ongoing fear of the enemies that might attack us and the evil that could befall us.

I don't mean to sound critical or judgmental here. We all face our share of fears. Honestly, there is a lot to be afraid of in this uncertain world. You might get fired. Or a loved one could get in a car wreck. Or a parent might be diagnosed with a terminal illness. Or your spouse could leave you. Or you might lose your home. Or the world could go to war. Or the stock market might crash. Or there could be an earthquake or a forest fire or a hurricane. Or . . . you fill in the blank.

What's the answer, then?

To embrace a faith in God that is big enough and honest enough to make space for trials and tragedies, not just for triumphs. A faith that doesn't just avoid pain but processes pain. A faith that works for real people in a real world. A faith that believes that no matter what happens—whether we live or die, win or lose, succeed or fail—God is in charge, and he can be trusted. Paul likely had this in mind when he wrote, "No, in all these things we are more than conquerors through him who loved us. For I am convinced that neither death nor life, neither angels nor demons, neither the present nor the future, nor any powers, neither height nor depth, nor anything else in all creation, will be able to separate us from the love of God that is in Christ Jesus our Lord" (Romans 8:37–39).

We're going to face some tough things from time to time, but none of them can break our relationship with God. Even if our worst fears come true, we can still count on God's love and presence. Isn't that what faith is all about? A childlike trust in the love of God?

When you learn to live with faith in God, death and loss lose their power. Faith enables you to face any threat, any bad news, any fear without being overwhelmed. Let faith define your life, and it will walk you through your death experiences unscathed. Don't only give it credit for the victories—let it carry you through failure, disappointment, and hurt too. That's when it is at its best.

If anything, faith in God is *energized* by death. It's like one of those superhero movies where someone can absorb the energy from an enemy's attack and then use it against them. When faith comes under attack, it only grows stronger.

Faith in God is not about ignoring personal responsibility or hiding from reality. Some people think faith is blind, but it's not. *Doubt* is blind. *Fear* is blind. Doubt and fear see things that aren't there and ignore things that are. They confuse the whole picture.

Faith, on the other hand, opens your eyes, not just to the physical world or your tangible circumstances but to the God who surrounds you with arms of love and armies of protection.

Yes, the worst might happen.

No, your miracle might not take place this side of heaven.

Yes, there are some difficult days ahead.

No, you might not get that bike or Sega Genesis for Christmas.

But you don't have to be afraid. You can be certain God is faithful in life and death because he's bigger than life and death. The grave couldn't hold him and death couldn't stop him.

The apostle Paul had this to say about living and dying: "If we live, we live for the Lord; and if we die, we die for the Lord. So, whether we live or die, we belong to the Lord" (Romans 14:8). That pretty much sums it up.

No matter what happens, we win.

FOUR

Mostly Dead Is
Slightly Alive

The classic movie *The Princess Bride* is a humorous love story that has never lost its popularity, because practically every line in it is quotable. In one scene, the main character, Wesley, has been tortured, and his friends are sure he's dead. They take him to see Miracle Max, a cynical miracle worker who has been driven underground by "the king's stinking son," as he puts it. The friends insist that Wesley is dead, to which Max replies sarcastically, "Whoo-hoo-hoo, look who knows so much. It just so happens that your friend here is only *mostly* dead. There's a big difference between mostly dead and all dead. Mostly dead is slightly alive. With all dead, well, with all dead there's usually only one thing you can do—go through his clothes and look for loose change."[1]

We've spent the last couple of chapters talking about how death is not the end and how faith in God can help us navigate death. Let's not get too funeral-happy, however. Too often we focus on the "mostly dead" state of whatever is bothering us: our finances, our careers, our investments, our love lives. But God and Miracle Max would like to point out that some of the things we think are dead are "slightly alive." Mostly dead and all dead might look the same sometimes, but they are two very different states of being. And it's important to be able to tell the difference.

Do you have a dream that you think is over and gone? Don't give up on it too quickly. It might be asleep. It might just be hibernating for a while. But maybe winter is almost over, and that dream is going to come roaring back to life.

Are you discouraged about a business idea you thought for sure was going to work, but the harder you try, the more things seem to go wrong? Talk to any entrepreneur out there, and they'll tell you the same thing—don't give up too soon.

Is there a relationship in your life that seems to have died? Maybe a best friend you fought with and are no longer speaking to, or a child who moved out of the house in anger and refuses to answer your calls, or a marriage that has been struggling for what seems like forever?

Don't write that person off just because you haven't seen signs of change lately. Unless God has made it clear that it's time to move on, wait a bit longer. I'm not saying you should force something, but don't be in a hurry to close a book if God is still writing the ending. Maybe he is doing something in that person's heart that you can't see.

Don't Be Afraid of Waking the Dead

Too often we try to prop up dead things and pretend they are just asleep, while we hold funerals for sleeping things because we assume they're dead. If something is truly dead, we should give it a proper burial and move on. But let's not bury something that is still alive. That's terrifying.

There is a town in Hertfordshire, England, named Braughing that celebrates a unique holiday called Old Man's Day every October 2.

On that date, back in 1571, a local resident named Mathew Wall passed away and was being carried in a processional to the cemetery. As the pallbearers walked down the road, one of them slipped on leaves that covered the ground, and the coffin crashed to the ground. Suddenly everyone heard banging from inside the coffin. The jolt had revived Mathew, who must have simply been unconscious for some unknown reason. They let him out, and he lived twenty-four more years.[2]

I can't even imagine the shock that people must have felt upon seeing the object of their mourning sitting up in a casket. Thankfully that's never happened in a funeral I've officiated, because I'm pretty sure that I and a few others in the congregation would have a heart attack on the spot. That's the stuff of horror movies. God knows I couldn't handle that.

My point is, let's not be too quick to declare something dead. Whether it's a dream, a project, a relationship, a business, a ministry, or a new way of living, give it time. Don't give up so quickly. Some of us are already filling out a death certificate for things that God is about to revive. Don't be that person.

> **Some of us are already filling out a death certificate for things that God is about to revive.**

I'm not telling you to ignore the reality of death. As I've already said, dealing with death and deathlike moments is the whole point of this book. We'll spend a lot of time burying things in the coming chapters. I would be remiss, though, to write about death without reminding you that God has a long history of overturning death at the last second. Sometimes after the last second.

The Bible tells the story of how one of Jesus' best friends, a man named Lazarus, became ill and passed away. When Jesus knew

Lazarus had died, he told his disciples, "Our friend Lazarus has fallen asleep; but I am going there to wake him up" (John 11:11).

His disciples replied, "Awesome, Jesus. That's great, but don't wake him up. If he sleeps, he'll get better." (That's my paraphrase.)

Jesus rolled his eyes. "Guys, it's a metaphor. He's actually dead. But I've got a surprise planned. Come on, let's go." (That's also my paraphrase, but I'm pretty sure the eye roll was accurate.) Then he went to Lazarus's tomb and raised him from the dead.

On another occasion the daughter of a synagogue leader had died, and Jesus said something similar: "The girl is not dead but asleep" (Matthew 9:24). Everyone laughed at that. So Jesus promptly kicked them out of the room. Sometimes you just have to get rid of the negative energy, right? Then Jesus took the little girl by the hand, and she came back to life.

In both instances Jesus called death "sleep." Why? Because for an eternal, all-powerful God, there isn't a bit of difference between sleep and death. Both are temporary. Both are reversible. Both are within his power to change. Yes, they really did die. But not for God. For him, it was just a matter of waking them back up.

In the same way, the little deaths of pain, loss, and suffering are not always as final as they might appear. Sometimes those things are just asleep, and God's alarm clock is about to go off. When they sit upright in their coffins, don't have a heart attack. That's just how God rolls.

Do You Need a Miracle or a Funeral?

Why do we struggle to know what is dead versus what is simply asleep?

Lots of reasons, probably. Sometimes we're discouraged. Sometimes we're tired. Sometimes we're ignorant. Sometimes we've

jumped to conclusions. Sometimes we're listening to the
wrong people. Sometimes we're
looking at faulty evidence.

Only you can really know
that for yourself, although it
will take some hard work and
brutal honesty to figure it out.

It's not my role to tell you
what is "mostly dead" and what
is "all dead." That's above my
pay grade. However, there are

> **That's life for you, isn't it? Always unpredictable. Occasionally traumatic. And ultimately safe in God's hands.**

a few questions I ask myself when I'm trying to figure out whether
something I wanted, dreamed of, prayed for, or expected is lying on
its deathbed, and I have to figure out whether it needs a miracle—or
a funeral.

1. *How important is this thing to me?*

   God cares about what we care about. When we follow
   him, we find ourselves caring about what he cares about. Our
   cares are connected. So if something is deeply important to
   you and doesn't show any signs of diminishing, don't give up
   on it too quickly. It might be an indication that this is God's
   dream too. On the other hand, if God has pointed your heart
   elsewhere, maybe it's time to bury it and look toward the
   future.

2. *Why is it so important to me?*

   This points to motivation. Is this thing giving you security or identity that should come from a healthier place? Is it
   propping up your ego? Is it preserving bitterness? Is it covering up sin? Is it a reflection of pride, stubbornness, anger,
   or some other less-than-noble motivation? Sometimes death

experiences are needed because they separate us from things that have taken on an unhealthy role in our lives. If you can identify and address problematic root issues, it will be much easier to decide whether something is supposed to remain in your life.

3. *Do I have realistic expectations?*

Nothing will frustrate you quicker than having wrong expectations. That's why putting together IKEA furniture is so exasperating. The box makes it look so easy, but trust me, it never is. Whether it's a work project, a romantic relationship, raising a child, writing a book, or a new product you're launching, getting an accurate picture of the complications you'll face is essential. Sometimes what we think is the agony of death is just the reality of life.

4. *Am I open to God's creativity?*

After Jesus' disciples had fished all night with no luck, Jesus told them to try throwing their nets off "the other side" of the boat. That command gets funnier the longer you think about it, especially since these guys were professional fishermen, and fish don't really operate in terms of "sides." Yet it worked. Before giving up on something, check in with God one more time. Ask for divine creativity and grace to see unexpected solutions.

5. *Where is the grace?*

The word *grace* often refers to mercy or compassion; but in the Bible, it goes beyond that. Grace is God's empowerment to do something. He gives us grace to love difficult people, grace to go through hard times, grace to give generously. That doesn't mean those things are easy, but they are *possible*. When it comes to whatever area of pain or loss you are evaluating, do you feel grace to let it go? Or do you have grace to pick it up and keep trying? Learn to let grace lead.

It's in God's Hands

Ultimately, of course, only God can determine whether a miracle or a funeral is in order. No matter how sure you are that something is dead, God might bring it back to life. And even when you are convinced that something should come to life, God might want it to rest in peace. That's why we must always hold everything in an open hand.

The story of Job is the ultimate biblical example of this kind of humble trust. After losing all his possessions, his income, and even his children, Job said, "The Lord gave and the Lord has taken away; may the name of the Lord be praised" (Job 1:21).

That's an incredible response. I'm 100 percent certain I would not have been that chill.

You know what's even more amazing? By the end of the story, God had given Job much more than he originally lost. When Job had it all, he lost it. And after he lost it all, he received it again.

That's life for you, isn't it? Always unpredictable. Occasionally traumatic. And ultimately safe in God's hands.

FIVE

Death Is Sacred

Parents of babies usually have a specific look about them (and smell, but we won't go there). It's a sort of silent, sleep-deprived, coffee-fueled desperation. Luckily that lasts only a few months, or at most a year or two. Unless they have another baby in that time, in which case the cycle starts over.

I get it. My wife and I have one son—an energetic, creative, awesome little guy named Maxwell. I can remember laying him down for the night when he was a baby, tiptoeing out of the room, and crawling into bed—only to hear, four minutes later, creepy howls piercing the stillness like something out of *The Hound of the Baskervilles*. I would stagger into the other room, grumbling under my breath about whoever came up with the phrase "sleep like a baby," pick the little dude up in my arms, and start the process over.

But at some point my wife and I had to let him cry himself to sleep. I'm not talking abuse or abandonment, of course. We knew he was fed, clean, warm, and safe—he was just exhausted. So were we. That's why we would let him cry for a few minutes until he finally drifted off into oblivion.

Those minutes felt like hours, though. If you're a parent, you know what I mean. Hearing his cries broke our hearts. Why? Because parents are hardwired to take care of their kids. Their children's pain awakens compassion, even when their "pain" is just a stubborn refusal to close their eyes and give in to sleep.

In the same way, our pain resonates in the heart of God.

Even if that pain is relatively small. Even if our suffering is partly our own fault. Even when we're exaggerating or being dramatic. Even when we're being selfish. Even when it's for our own good. Even when God knows it's about to end and something better is coming.

God always cares, and he is always close.

Sorrow Is Holy Ground

God empathizes with our pain. *Empathy* is the capacity to comprehend and share the feelings of someone else. That describes God perfectly. He's not some disconnected, aloof taskmaster in the sky who only cares about how much we get done or whether we've sinned today. He cares about us. He understands what we are going through, and he shares our emotions.

The Bible frequently talks about how God "hears our cries" or "sees our suffering" (e.g., Psalm 106:44). The little deaths we go through move the heart of God. This is the part of loss and disappointment that we often overlook. He isn't only the God we pray to before loss happens, when we are asking for a miracle. He's also the God we find refuge in after the sting of death, when nothing seems to make sense. As I mentioned earlier, we are infinitely valuable to him, so he shares our pain. Even if it's a relatively small loss in the eyes of other people—maybe you were passed over for a promotion, or your car was broken into, or you received a rejection letter from a publisher, or a family pet died—these death experiences are important to God.

God knows the future, but his foreknowledge doesn't make him callous to our suffering in the present. In the previous chapter, we talked about the death of Lazarus. Before Jesus raised him from the dead, he first met with Lazarus's sisters, Martha and Mary. They were brokenhearted, of course. Even angry. You can hear it in their words in John 11. At one point, when Jesus saw the grief of Mary and the others, he was overcome with compassion and began to weep.

Do you realize how much that says about God's heart? Jesus knew he was going to raise Lazarus from the dead. He knew the sorrow of Mary and Martha would become joy in a matter of hours, maybe minutes. So when he saw their grief, he could have responded, "Where's your faith? Where's your gratitude? Be strong! Stop whining and just trust God."

Instead, he wept. Think about that. Their pain mattered to him. He didn't ignore the loss; he validated it. He sat with them in their suffering and he shared their tears.

Why? Why would our tears matter to God?

It's simple. Because *we* matter to God. And not just our productivity, or our holiness, or our generosity.

Our loss matters.

Our pain matters.

Our anger matters.

Our anxiety matters.

Our confusion matters.

Our disappointment matters.

One of Israel's ancient songs says, "Precious in the sight of the LORD is the death of his faithful servants" (Psalm 116:15). The psalmist was talking about literal death here, but the principle also applies to the metaphorical death we suffer when we lose something important to us. "Precious" means it has value. Pain, loss, betrayal, abandonment, failure, sickness, and all the other death experiences we've been looking at are not a light matter to God but rather something he takes seriously.

God not only sees your tears but is moved by them. When you weep, he weeps. If you are going through pain and grief, imagine Jesus mourning with you. Visualize his embrace as you cry, argue, or vent. He's not judging you—he's holding you. As Irish poet and playwright Oscar Wilde wrote, "Where there is sorrow there is holy ground."[1]

Your pain is precious. Your grief is holy. Your loss is sacred.

When death strikes, don't be in a hurry to stifle your grief. Don't gaslight yourself into silence. Don't gloss over your loss in the name of faith or strength. Let yourself "feel all the feels" for as long as you need, because your death moments are precious in the sight of the Lord.

God Is Holding Your Heart

David, the ancient king of Israel who wrote many of the psalms, said this about God: "The LORD is close to the brokenhearted and saves those who are crushed in spirit" (Psalm 34:18). Specifically, God has a soft spot for people in pain.

Jesus' years of ministry showed this same heart for the hurting. If you read through the Gospels, you'll find him with the rejects, the outcasts, the poor, the sick, the forgotten, the lonely, the addicted, the angry, the disenfranchised, the oppressed, and the misunderstood. Being close to people who were suffering (and *helping* those people) was his literal job description.

In times of loss God seems to reveal himself in a special way. It's as if he is somehow more present and more real in the storm than he is in the calm. I'm sure that is due in part to how we are more alert and desperate during hard times, but I'm convinced it goes beyond that. The Jesus I read about in the Bible always seemed ready to drop everything to serve those in pain. More than two thousand years later, he still does the same thing.

I shared earlier what it was like to lose my father at a young age and how I felt at the time. But I also remember hearing my mom tell me how she felt after losing her life partner, her best friend, her husband, and the father of her children. She sat down with us and said, "Although he's gone, it's almost like God has wrapped his hands around my heart and shielded me from the pain that I am supposed to feel."

It's not that she had an absence of pain. Rather, she could identify the presence of God in that pain. She told us that she had never felt the closeness of God like she did then.

To this day I marvel at her strength. I am amazed by her endurance and her willpower to continue to move forward in faith and love. Although things would never be the same, she accepted the challenge to live to the fullest every single day. That strength was born out of the closeness and presence of God in a season of great loss.

God is not far away in times of death. In fact, he's closer than ever in these times. That nearness should inspire comfort, not fear or shame. If your view of God usually involves him being mad at you for something you've done, you need to get a new view of God. That's not the way Jesus treated people, which means it's not the way God treats people. Especially when they are suffering.

If you're going through some sort of loss or pain, some death experience, let God draw close to heal you. Remember, he is not shaming you or blaming you. He's not pointing out all the things you could have done differently or telling you this is all your fault. He's not punishing you by taking away something that was precious to you. He's not taking off points for how little faith you have or making notes about whether you handle pain the right way, as if this were some test of your faith.

Sure, there might be some things you should have done differently or some areas that need to improve. God will get to that later. A funeral is not the time to talk about what should have been done in the past or what needs to be done in the future. A funeral is a time to mourn. A time to remember that grief is important and sorrow matters. A time to recognize the sacredness of both life and death.

> **You do have to move past death, but you don't have to skip the funeral.**

Of course, I'm not saying to live with grief forever. Eventually the funeral ends and everybody leaves. Life must continue. If you try to set up a tent next to the grave and camp out there forever, you'll be asked to leave. And if you insist on staying, you'll probably get arrested.

You do have to move past death, but you don't have to skip the funeral. After all, that's where Jesus is. He's there not just to dry your tears but to shed a few of his own. Like a best friend, he'll sit with you for however long you need. And, when you're ready, he'll be there beside you as you face the next stage of life.

SIX

Honestly Speaking

When I was about six years old, my parents bought a goldfish for my sisters and me. We named him David. As far as fish go, David was a rather active fellow, and we loved to watch him. He would swim super rapidly and suddenly stop right before he smashed into the small glass tank he called home.

One day after school I noticed David was swimming more slowly than usual. I thought maybe he was sick or had eaten too much, because he was not acting like the David I knew. Then the week after that, I noticed David had developed a small black spot on the left side of his body. He was swimming better again, though, so I didn't worry too much about the spot. The following week the black spot on his left side was mysteriously gone, and now his back fin was a lot more prominent than it had been the week before. It was a miracle how fast and beautiful that fin had grown.

A few weeks later I came home from school one day and went to check on David. To my shock he was inside a plastic bag in the fish tank. I was intrigued, so I went looking for my mom. When I found her, I asked, "Mom, why is David in a bag?"

She looked at me like she had just seen a ghost. She reluctantly told me that David had gone to fishy heaven. (Later I would find out that "fishy heaven" was our toilet.) She then told me that this wasn't the second David. Or even the third David. As a matter of fact, nearly every week since we had come home with the original David, they had to buy a new one because the old one would die.

Goldfish have a life span of ten to fifteen years. But each David died prematurely because the tank was too small. By artificially keeping "David" alive, my parents were protecting what was killing him in the first place. It would have been better to address the death, deal with the fallout, and make the changes needed so that David 2.0 could have lived to a ripe old age.

> **You can't heal what you won't deal with, and you can't deal with what you won't admit.**

I'm a parent now, so I understand why they wouldn't want their children to have to deal with the death of a beloved pet. It must have seemed easier to keep buying new Davids than to address death. Denying the problem didn't solve it, however—it only postponed it. Actually it made it even worse. This brings us to an important point: you can't heal what you won't deal with, and you can't deal with what you won't admit.

Denial Is Not a Solution

Parents aren't the only ones who try to deny death. Often we do this to *ourselves*. We are unwilling to recognize the things in our lives that are dead. But if we are not honest about those things, if we keep trying to pretend "I'm good, you're good, we're all good," then our pain will end up only growing. It won't go away just because we insist that death hasn't happened. It will just go deeper into our souls. Once there it will often fester, turning into things like bitterness, unbelief, depression, and hatred.

This is where honesty comes in. You have to be willing to admit when something is broken, lost, toxic, or wrong. Rather than defending it or disguising it, you have to bury it. Maybe it's an addiction that's slowly tearing apart your marriage or a relationship that needs to end. It could be a dream that was never meant to be or bitterness frowm a past hurt. Perhaps it's an area of selfishness or pride that you've never yielded to God. Whatever it is, stop denying that death has happened. Give it a proper funeral, then leave it in the past.

In 1969, psychiatrist Elisabeth Kübler-Ross published a book titled *On Death and Dying* that outlined what she called the five stages of grief: denial, anger, bargaining, depression, and acceptance. She based her work on conversations with hundreds of terminally ill patients. In her experience, people would typically go through these stages, often in this order, after they received their initial diagnosis.

In the more than fifty-plus years since her book was published, the five stages of grief have become a widely used way to think about the complex reactions triggered by all types of loss and grief. In my own life, grief often manifests in these ways. Not all five stages occur every time or in that order, but they definitely show up often.

Notice what comes first in Kübler-Ross's model: *denial*. Often our first reaction to death experiences is to deny them. The fact that we have lost, or are about to lose, something near and dear to us is so painful that we prefer to stick our heads in the sand and act as though nothing has happened.

"No, that's impossible. There's no way. I don't believe it. I can't believe it. There must be something else I can do."

It feels easier to *deny* death than to *process* death, but denial isn't a sustainable solution. You can play pretend only for so long. Eventually you have to admit that what you loved—your boyfriend, your job, the business you started, the house you've been dreaming of building, the goldfish you bought your kid—is gone, and it's not coming back.

Maybe the dead thing is something you used to have, but you lost it. Or maybe it's something you've been pursuing for years, and you've finally realized it's never going to happen. Whatever the case, there comes a moment when you find yourself in front of the open casket, staring death in the face. That's when the finality of death gets real.

It's a solemn moment. A sad moment. And as we saw in the last chapter, a sacred moment.

Four Ways to Be Honest with Yourself

God is not afraid of honesty. If you doubt me, just read the Psalms. God expects us to be transparent. He responds to it. He can work with it. Remember when the disciples thought Lazarus was only asleep? Once Jesus realized they weren't aware of the seriousness of the situation, the Bible says, "So then he told them plainly, 'Lazarus is dead'" (John 11:14). Jesus wasn't going to perpetuate some illusion just to keep them from being sad. They had to face death before they could see beyond it.

It's worth asking ourselves, *Why is it so hard to accept death?* When it comes to goldfish and kids, the answer is obvious: to avoid a nuclear meltdown of grief. Spending twenty-five cents a week to keep the illusion of life intact is a small price to pay for peace and harmony in the home. But why do we lie to ourselves? I don't pretend to have all the answers to that question. The human psyche is complex and often illogical. I would, however, like to share a few strategies to overcome denial and be honest with yourself.

Remember that faith and honesty go together.

Sometimes we think that true faith never gives up, backs down, or lets go. Since we often assume death is defeat, we deny it to prop up our faith. Denial is not faith, though. It might even be fear or pride.

Actually *honesty* is a manifestation of faith. One of the most faith-filled things you can do is admit that you are hurt, confused, and angry. On the other hand, one of the most doubt-filled things you can do is sweep your feelings under the rug and pretend you're fine.

Once a blind man called out to Jesus for a miracle. It was clear what he needed, but Jesus asked him anyway. "What do you want me to do for you?" (Luke 18:41).

The man didn't pretend things were fine. He was honest and direct: "Lord, I want to see."

Jesus responded, "Receive your sight; your faith has healed you" (v. 42). The man's honesty and faith weren't in contradiction—they were connected.

Honesty proves that you are confident enough in God to ask hard questions and feel difficult emotions. It is a sign that your trust is in him, not in your own power, logic, or resources. Acknowledging death doesn't undermine your faith; it points you to faith and proves your faith.

Override your instinct to ignore reality.

If we've believed something or worked toward something for a long time, it can be difficult to change. Why? First, because nobody likes to be proven wrong. That's hard on the ego. And second, because it makes all our work and sacrifice feel like they were in vain.

Psychologically speaking, our minds often prefer to reinterpret reality than to admit that something we are so invested in is wrong or dead. This is just our brains trying to do their job, which is to protect us. *Accepting death is painful*, our subconscious reasons, *so to avoid pain, let's deny death. What could possibly go wrong?*

So we buy another David and restock the fishbowl. And nothing changes.

The good news? You can override your brain. Don't give in to the temporary relief of denial. It won't solve anything, and it will ultimately make things worse.

Align your mind and emotions.

Maybe you've heard the phrase, "Sometimes your heart needs more time to accept what your mind already knows." There's a lot of truth to that. If your emotions are raw, you might need to take a little time to process them before moving on. It's one thing to accept something mentally, but it's another to walk through the complex emotions involved.

The opposite is also true: sometimes your mind needs more time to accept what your heart already knows. You might know something needs to be buried without being able to explain it logically. In that case, don't be too quick to dismiss your feelings as "just emotions." Your reasoning might need some time to catch up with your emotions.

Humans are complicated, multifaceted beings. We can't separate our minds from our hearts. They work together—and sometimes they fight together. The trick is to value and listen to both of them until you figure out what is true.

Embrace the future even when it's not what you expected.

This is a big one. Facing a reality that no longer includes a certain person, job, or dream can feel overwhelming. We wonder, *How can I go on? And why would I even want to? If this were to die, would I ever love again? Laugh again? Hope again?* So rather than accepting death and moving forward, we try to stay in the past.

Don't let fear of the future keep you from dealing with the present. That only postpones the inevitable. As I said earlier, with God, death isn't just an ending; it's also a new beginning. We have to remember that and then reimagine the future.

Disappointment is not a destination; it's a doorway. We walk through it in faith, trusting that there will be peace and joy and good on the other side, just as there was on this side.

Honesty Is Worth It

Just like any habit, learning to be honest about your struggles, fears, and failures takes practice. There's an art to it that is more difficult than you might think. Being authentic with your death experiences, though, will help you overcome the things that hold you back, and it will give God space to turn your endings into beginnings. Honesty is always the first step toward healing.

Life has a lot of disappointment in it—a lot of little deaths. It's okay to admit that. I would say it's *healthy* to admit that. But we don't stay forever in a place of loss and lament. Instead, we hold figurative funerals. We process our losses by recognizing them, grieving them, and saying goodbye to them. We lay to rest our lost hopes, our broken dreams, our failed projects, our shattered relationships. We do this respectfully and carefully—but we do it firmly too. Our disappointments must become part of our past.

How about you? Are you carrying something you need to set down? Propping something up that needs to be laid to rest? Performing CPR on something that flatlined years ago? Have you been replacing your Davids every week and pretending nothing is dead, rather than figuring out what needs to change? If so, maybe it's time for that funeral. Honesty might be painful in the moment, but it will be worth it in the end.

That's the goal of the next section, actually: to pinpoint the things that need to be laid to rest. After we pause to think about the reflection questions that follow this chapter, we're going to look at six areas of our lives that might need a funeral: relationships, dreams, security, control, sin, and certainty. Each of these represents a potential ending that God can transform into a beginning.

> **Honesty might be painful in the moment, but it will be worth it in the end.**

I believe with all my heart that God has a better future for you. That might be difficult to believe now, especially if you're mourning the loss of something dear to you, but it will become clearer with time. I'm not saying it will be a painless process—death hurts like hell itself. It's an enemy, an aberration, a thief. However, there is life after death. If you're willing to let the right things die, you'll discover life on the other side.

Part I: A Matter of Life and Death

QUESTIONS FOR REFLECTION

Chapter 1. Butter Beans and Fried Chicken

1. Is it difficult for you to take time to recognize what you've lost? Do you tend to move on too quickly? Why or why not?
2. What does overcoming look like to you when you are going through times of loss, grief, or pain?
3. What does "letting go" mean to you? How can letting go help you overcome in difficult seasons?

Chapter 2. Endings Are Beginnings

1. How does the thought of physical death make you react? Do you think that's a healthy way to view death?
2. How do "little deaths" (the losses and pain you face from time to time) make you feel? Do you think that's a healthy way to view those situations?
3. Does knowing that Jesus conquered death itself help you face the little deaths of life? In what ways?

Chapter 3. Faith in the Dark

1. How would you define *faith*?
2. How do difficult times affect your faith (both positively and negatively)?
3. How does faith help you deal with fear? Can you think of a time when you were able to face something difficult because of your confidence in God?

Chapter 4. Mostly Dead Is Slightly Alive

1. Do you tend to give up on dreams or projects too easily? Or consider the other extreme: Do you hold on to them for too long? What results has this caused for you?
2. How do you decide when to give up on something and when to persevere?
3. Can you think of a time when something you thought was over or dead actually wasn't, and it ended up being an important part of your life? In what ways did God use it to affect you positively after its "resurrection"?

Chapter 5. Death Is Sacred

1. How would you define or describe *empathy*?
2. What do you think God feels when you go through hard times?
3. Can you think of a time when your suffering or loss drew you closer to God or taught you something important about him? In what ways?

Chapter 6. Honestly Speaking

1. Have you ever tried to deny that something was lost or broken in your life? How did that work out?

Questions for Reflection

2. In hard times, how can you be both honest and full of faith? Is this difficult for you?
3. Have you ever had to readjust to a future you didn't expect? How did you handle that process? That is, what worked and what didn't work?

PART II

Processional

Confrontation

The processional is about recognizing what has been lost and allowing grief to be felt and embraced. In the following chapters we will focus on recognizing and accepting the things in our lives that have died. We are going to walk through six different "death experiences" or "little deaths," as we've been calling them: specific areas where we might be facing loss, pain, or disappointment. Think of this as a moment to acknowledge what has been lost, pay your respects, and begin to find closure.

It's hot outside—the sticky, heavy heat of summer in the South—but the church is cool and dark. Music plays softly while people walk into the sanctuary and search for an empty seat among the rows of pews, stopping along the way to greet old friends in respectful whispers. At the front of the room, lined along the altar, bouquets of flowers spill their fragrance into the air.

The double doors at the back of the church swing open and golden daylight floods in. Instantly a hush falls over the room and the congregation stands. The pastor enters first, dressed in a black suit and carrying a Bible. Behind him six pallbearers walk up the church steps and through the doors, bearing a mahogany casket on their shoulders.

The congregants watch the casket go by, silently paying their respects to the deceased. Next the family walks down the aisle, also dressed in black. Their faces are somber but at peace, and they nod their muted gratitude to a few members of the congregation as they file past.

The pallbearers carefully lower the casket onto a stand at the front of the church as the family is seated in the front rows. The spouse of the deceased is crying softly, and the sound brings tears to the eyes of those in the room. Hovering in the air is an unspoken sense of finality, a consciousness that things will never be the way they were before.

On behalf of the family, the pastor thanks everyone for coming, then opens in prayer. The ritual is comforting, but his words don't change the fact that there is a casket behind him, an unmistakable symbol of death and loss that draws the focus and elicits grief.

This is an ending. A last chapter. There is no denying it, no softening it. All there can be is acceptance, and remembrance, and faith.

It's time to confront specific death experiences carefully yet courageously and honestly. As we noted before, honesty is the first step toward healing. Here's the thing, though: Nobody else can be honest for you. You have to do this for yourself.

So I invite you to reflect on your own experiences in six important areas: saying goodbye to *people* you care about, recovering from shattered *dreams*, staying calm when you lose your sources of *security*, trusting in God even when things seem out of your *control*, putting to death issues of *sin*, and navigating the loss of *certainty*. In one (or more) of these areas, you might be dealing with deep loss, and I encourage you to give yourself space to think through how that is affecting you and how you should respond.

Remember, you don't have to process the disappointments and deaths you face alone. Let God have your endings. Give him the raw pain, the deep confusion, the seething anger, the profound loss. He is the only one truly capable of healing your soul. In his grace and goodness and love, he'll transform what you thought was an ending into a precious beginning.

SEVEN

The Worst Hurt: Losing People

When I was in the sixth grade, I had a crush on a girl in my class. For weeks I mulled over the idea of asking her to be my girlfriend, trying to muster up the courage to ask her out.

Finally I wrote her a note. At the top it said, "Do you like me?" Beneath that I put three options with little boxes to check off. I'm sure you can guess what they were: yes, no, and maybe.

I watched as she read the note, then, without a word, folded it up and put it in her pocket. Over the next few days, I saw her in and out of class, but she never said anything to me. I waited anxiously for her response, hoping it would be a yes. The silence continued. At this point even a "maybe" would have been acceptable.

More days went by. Then, one day, the note appeared in my locker. I unfolded it as fast as I could. To my dismay, there was a giant X in the "no" box.

I was devastated, of course. I went from having a crush to being crushed. Because I was so heartbroken, I soon began telling my friends that I didn't even like her, that I didn't want her to be my girlfriend. That's sixth-grade logic for you.

It's crazy how deeply we can feel things like rejection and betrayal, isn't it? We can go from obsessing over someone to wanting to cut them out of our lives completely. It's like one of those mafia movies where someone is backstabbed by a friend or family member they trusted, and they growl that famous line, "You're dead to me now." There is something about the vulnerability and connection involved in building a relationship that makes the loss of that relationship hurt deeply. Of all the little deaths we go through in life, *losing people* may be the most difficult of all.

It's So Hard to Say Goodbye

Losing people to death, abandonment, life change, or any other circumstance is difficult and painful. It's a form of death, whether they are still physically alive or not. Their absence creates a death experience that can have a deep impact on you.

- A boyfriend who broke up with you
- A wife who walked out on you
- A son who ran away from home
- A daughter who passed away
- A friend who took their own life
- A mother who never loved you
- A father who abandoned your family
- A best friend who betrayed you
- A family member who abused you
- An authority figure who manipulated or silenced you

If any of those bring back painful memories, I'm so sorry. Again, relationship losses are deeply painful, and even years later, they have the power to awaken feelings of hurt, fear, rejection, and anger. If you dig into your past and think of the things you lost that hurt the most, my guess is that *people* will occupy all the top spots on that list. Yes, it hurts to lose a house, a job, a cell phone, a wallet, a business opportunity, a car, or some other material thing—but those are all replaceable. People are not. So when we are abandoned, betrayed, abused, silenced, ignored, or left behind, it cuts incredibly deep.

Even when the loss wasn't something done to us intentionally, it still hurts. For example, if a friend or loved one moves away or dies, it leaves a hole in our hearts. When a child grows up and leaves the home to begin life as an adult, we experience a bittersweet feeling of excitement mixed with loss. When someone makes a decision that ends up having negative consequences for us, we feel the pain of being collateral damage. We might not blame any of these people, but the loss we experience still leaves a wound.

Why does it hurt so badly when our loss is connected to people? First, because we allowed ourselves to be open and vulnerable. This is a good and necessary part of relationships, of course. We can't love without being vulnerable. So we opened our hearts, let our guards down, and let people in. We dreamed together and built together. They saw our hopes and fears, our strengths and weaknesses, our victories and failures. We showed our true selves to them, thinking they were a safe place. Then they betrayed us. They broke our trust, and we'll never be able to see them the same way again. Even if it was not an intentional act, it can still *feel* like betrayal, though we know life is more to blame than they are. When we let someone into our hearts, it is always painful to see them go.

Second, we hurt because the loss feels personal. That makes sense if you think about it. We are talking about *persons*, so whatever they do is, by definition, personal. If a bird flies overhead, and suddenly you feel something wet and goopy dripping down your neck, you might be upset and grossed out, but you don't take it personally. You were in the wrong place at the wrong time. (Unless birds really *can* aim, which I don't think we can fully rule out.) When it's a person who has hurt you, though—especially if it was intentional—it's almost impossible not to get your feelings hurt. I think it's those nuances of intentionality and broken trust that make relational hurt the worst kind of hurt.

You know how this feels, I'm sure. You're familiar with the emotions and thoughts that rush in after you are wounded by someone you trusted. *How could they do that to me? What did I ever do to them? This isn't fair. They are horrible. Terrible. Awful. I hate them. I hope they pay for what they've done to me.*

Our thoughts get very dark, very quickly. We don't just feel hurt; we feel attacked. They are the aggressors and we are the victims. They are the bad guys and we are the good guys. This binary, them-versus-us approach is too simplistic, however, and it tends to do more harm than good. We need a better approach to the dead and dying relationships we've experienced.

After all, relationships can cause us deep pain, but they can also bring us the greatest blessings. That's why it's so important to bury the things that should remain in the past rather than hang on to them. We don't want past betrayal, abandonment, or abuse to affect our future relationships.

How to See Dead People

How then should we treat the people who have broken our hearts, dreams, or bank accounts? How should we look at dead people? Not ghosts, obviously—I mean the people whose absence is causing us pain, whether that absence is due to physical separation (such as literal death or moving to a new city) or to some change in our relationship (maybe because of a conflict, a romantic breakup, or abandonment). When we think of the people we've lost, how do we see them, think about them, remember them?

Relational conflict in general is an enormous topic, so I'm not going to attempt to deal with it here. Instead, I want to focus on the death aspect of this topic—relational *loss*.

> **Suffering is a personal journey, one nobody else can live for you.**

How do we process the pain that comes from being abandoned or hurt by someone we trusted?

As with all grief, I can't totally answer that for you. Suffering is a personal journey, one nobody else can live for you. I do have a few thoughts that I'd like to share, though. These are things that have helped me process difficult relationship moments.

Recognize both the good and the bad.

When someone hurts us deeply, our instinct is to vilify and villainize them. We want to make them the ultimate, absolute bad guys in our narratives. Generally, I think we react this way when the people who hurt us knew exactly what they were doing; however, we might also do it if the hurt was unintentional or careless. Turning the people who wounded us into villains seems like it should make the pain easier to take. If they are evil, then we can hate them. And if we can hate them, we don't have to feel so hurt by them. So the logic goes, anyway. But it's a false logic. Hatred doesn't heal pain; it just buries it alive. Sooner or later, like a zombie in a horror movie, it comes back to stalk us.

Instead of villainizing people, realize that they—like us—are a mix of good and bad. Nobody is all evil, and nobody is all good. We all need some grace from time to time.

That doesn't mean we excuse their wrong actions or try to get them back into our lives. It simply means we can remember the good times, too, not just the bad. It means we don't have to erase their contribution to who we are or the memories we share.

Remember that everybody is the hero in their own story.

I don't say this to justify abuse or aggression. All I'm saying is that from the perspectives of those who hurt us, they might have *felt* justified. In their minds they probably downplayed their guilt and exaggerated their virtues.

How do I know that? Because we all do this. It's one reason Jesus told us not to try to pluck a speck from someone else's eye if we have a plank embedded in our own (Luke 6:41–42). We all tend to hype up the purity of our hearts while slandering our enemies. We give ourselves all the benefit of the doubt, and we give them none of it. The only way to overcome that tendency is to choose to love our enemies. Again, I'm just quoting Jesus.

Acknowledging that people who have hurt us might think they are the good guys is difficult. It might lead us to ask uncomfortable questions: *What if there is some truth in their perspective? What if we share some of the blame? What if they aren't quite as evil as we told ourselves they were?* Those are scary thoughts. Humanizing our aggressors might end up invalidating or even prolonging our hurt—or so our mental self-defense system tries to tell us. In reality, trying to see from their perspective helps us heal from hurt by awaking our compassion and humility, two qualities that go a long way toward eliminating pain.

Even in our hurt, we must remain empathetic, humble, and willing to show mercy.

Reclaim your autonomy and agency.

Simply put, don't remain a victim. *Autonomy* means the freedom to make your own choices, and *agency* means the ability to act. As a human made in the image of God, you deserve both. You have free will (autonomy) and freedom (agency).

The problem with loss and pain (especially when it's caused by abuse) is that it tends to paralyze us, or at least limit us. Things like fear, bitterness, and trauma can chip away at how we see ourselves. You might have been victimized by someone, but that doesn't have to become your identity. You are a person first, not a victim. You are a child of God, loved and valued by him, saved by grace, full of potential, called to greatness, and chosen for a purpose. Don't let the terrible actions of other people or the tragedies of life redefine you.

How do you recover autonomy and agency? Start by focusing on what God says about you in the Bible. In particular, notice how Jesus restored dignity and humanity to everyone he met. Pain and rejection will try to define you, but don't listen to them. God sees you as so much more than your suffering.

When you listen to God's voice, you'll find yours.

Choose to forgive.

This is a tough one, but part of the reason why is because we often buy into a false view of forgiveness. Forgiveness does not mean ignoring what the person did to you, excusing their wrong behavior, or giving them infinite do-overs. Too often forgiveness has been used as a tool to abuse, silence, and control people.

Instead, forgiveness is about releasing your responsibility to judge or punish the other person. You forgive them by giving them to God, the ultimate judge and the only one capable and holy enough to actually do justice. Paul wrote, "Do not take revenge, my dear friends, but leave room for God's wrath, for it is written: 'It is mine to avenge; I will repay,' says the Lord" (Romans 12:19).

Forgiveness is about you, not them. It is finding peace in your heart. When you forgive someone, you stop wasting emotional energy on trying to fully resolve, understand, or undo something that should be left behind. Forgiveness is your choice, which makes it a powerful way to reclaim your agency and autonomy.

Forgiveness may include pursuing tangible justice, by the way. When Paul said "leave room for God's wrath," he meant don't seek *revenge*. You can still seek apologies, justice, freedom, change, and restitution, if those things are needed or helpful.

Seek professional help.

By *seek professional help* I mean anybody whose education and experience are designed to address your specific situation. That might mean therapy, family counseling, legal advice, government agencies, nonprofits, or even the police. No matter what you're going through, faith in God *does not* mean you have to stick things out alone. Find people to help. Faith works best in community, and wisdom is available for the asking.

By the way, if you are in a dangerous situation, please don't stay there. The Bible says that "God has called us to live in peace" (1 Corinthians 7:15), and that instruction was given specifically in the context of family conflict. Peace and safety are basic needs, and you shouldn't allow anyone to tell you otherwise.

If you're struggling with the loss of a loved one in the past, or if you're dealing with a person who is causing ongoing pain and suffering for you or your family, do whatever it takes to pursue peace. I say that with all the love and concern I have. God wants to help you find freedom, so don't stay silent or fight alone.

Yes, No, Maybe

When my sixth-grade crush squashed my romantic aspirations, I had a choice to make. Ironically, I faced the same three options I had written down on that note: yes, no, maybe.

Yes, I'll recover and move on.

No, I'll never recover, and instead I'll spiral into adolescent angst forever.

Maybe I'll recover, but I need some time to process, think, and heal.

I'd like to suggest something. If someone has hurt you deeply, instead of jumping straight to the "yes" option and instantly trying to feel better, or instead of quickly choosing the "no" option and declaring that angst is now your best friend forever, what if you left that choice at "maybe" for a little while? My crush held on to my note for days before she made a decision. She made the wrong one, of course, and she likely regrets it to this day (okay, that's unlikely). But at least she was honest enough to not rush into a decision. Either that or she enjoyed making me suffer. Or maybe she forgot entirely until she found the note at the bottom of her locker. There are a lot of options here, I suppose. But you get my point: she didn't rush her response, and neither should you.

You should take time to work through relational loss because the people who are gone truly matter. They matter to you, they matter to God, and they matter to the world. At the same time, *you* matter. Your loss is real and your pain is valid. You don't have to pretend you have it all figured out right out of the gate. When it comes to losing people, there are some things you might never figure out. Who was right? Who was wrong? Who hurt whom, and why? How? You might not ever fully know.

The "maybe" option should eventually turn into the "yes" option, of course. For your own mental and emotional well-being, work through what you can understand and leave what you can't under-stand in the past. But you don't have to do that overnight, and you don't have to do it alone. As I said earlier, you can always seek help from people who know better than you how to deal with the trauma of loss, abandonment, abuse, betrayal, and death.

Before we move on to the next funeral on the schedule, take a few moments to think back over the people who have done you wrong over the years. How are you doing with those relationship deaths? Are any of the ghosts still haunting you? Is there trauma from abandonment or betrayal you need to address? Are there people you need to forgive? Is there any relational pain you need to process?

If so, don't feel like you have to "get over it" right now. That's probably not realistic or healthy. What you can do, though, is commit to making progress toward healing. That will take work, honesty, and time, but I promise you it will be worth it.

EIGHT

Sadly Ever After: Losing Dreams

Years ago, before I was married, I had the opportunity to take over a local hamburger restaurant. I renamed it Patty Shakes, and I immediately poured my heart and soul into building the business. It was a labor of love for me, and after a year or two of hard work, the restaurant began to do well. Eventually I even opened a second one. I was excited and full of dreams, and I just knew I was going to be the next Chick-fil-A.

But then the economy began to change. It became much harder to make the business work from a financial standpoint. Around that time I also met my wife, and a new season began for me. After wrestling with the decision for a long time, I finally admitted to myself that it was time to sell the restaurants. I hadn't accomplished what I wanted to. Deep inside I felt like I had failed.

One day I was talking to a mentor of mine, and it came up in conversation. He asked, "Tim, why do you feel like a failure?"

"Because I had to sell the business."

He looked at me for a moment. "Well, did you learn anything?"

"Yes," I replied. "I learned a lot."

"Okay then, so why do you feel like a failure?"

I said it again: "Because I had to sell the business."

He replied, "Let me teach you a valuable lesson. As long as you learn, you don't lose, and you're not a failure."

I realized then that sometimes what seems like failure is simply a lesson learned through experience. Yes, my dream had been lost. But that didn't mean *I* had lost. It simply meant a season was changing, and I needed to change with it. More importantly, in my new season, I needed to dare to dream again.

Have you ever had a dream that died? Maybe it was a business idea that you just knew would make you millions, and after pouring your blood, sweat, and tears into it for years, everything fell apart overnight. Or maybe it was a dream romance: You were dating a boyfriend or girlfriend who seemed to be the other half of a match made in heaven. But then things went downhill, you broke up, and now you're drinking LaCroix out of a coffee mug and listening to Taylor Swift on repeat.

When it comes to broken dreams, there are a million hypothetical scenarios we could talk about, but I'll stop before we all get depressed. The point is that sometimes we don't live happily ever after. Dreams don't always come true. And to be honest, some dreams *shouldn't* come true. But that doesn't make them hurt any less when they shatter in front of our eyes.

When this happens how do we respond? Do we try to put the pieces of our shattered hopes back together, like Humpty Dumpty? Do we shake our fists at fate and promise to get revenge? Do we blame our parents, partners, or random strangers? Do we spiral into depression, convinced that our happily ever after is now a sadly ever after, and that God is cruel, life sucks, and dreams never come true?

God Is the Original Dreamer

In a moment we'll get to some suggestions about how to handle broken dreams. But first let's talk about why dreams matter. Because whatever you do, you can't stop dreaming. That would be the biggest tragedy of all.

> **Whatever you do, you can't stop dreaming.**

Dreaming is a deeply human trait. It's in our nature to envision, to hope, and to imagine. We see opportunities and potential everywhere we look. We hope and dream so easily because we were made in the image of God, the ultimate dreamer. When we imagine doing great things, we reflect his nature. When we make plans and take steps to pursue those dreams, we are doing exactly what he designed us to do. God has set hope within our hearts.

Throughout the Bible we see God dropping dreams into people's hearts and minds. Sometimes these were literal dreams about their future; other times they were prophetic visions of what their future could be:

- Abraham and Sarah would have descendants like the stars of the sky (Genesis 12, 18).
- Hagar would be protected and blessed immeasurably (Genesis 16).
- Moses would deliver the Israelites from Egypt (Exodus 3).
- Deborah and Jael would defeat an enemy king (Judges 4).

- David would become king of Israel (1 Samuel 16).
- Mary would give birth to Jesus, the Savior (Luke 1).

Those people are well-known heroes in the Bible. Here's the thing, though. If you go back and read their stories, they had to go through a lot of hardship before the dream came true. Often the dream seemed impossible.

Abraham and Sarah were in their nineties and didn't have a child. How would they ever become parents of a multitude? Hagar was a slave, cast out into the desert to die. How could she become a nation? Moses was an exile hiding in the desert. How could he lead a nation of slaves to freedom? Deborah and Jael were women in a patriarchal world, not commanders or even soldiers. How could the battle be swayed by their actions? David was a shepherd boy with a gift for poetry. How could he ever become king? Mary was a single teenage girl. How could she become the mother of God himself?

There are hundreds more stories like these in the Bible. God inspired people of all backgrounds and abilities to believe for the impossible: men and women, rich and poor, young and old, Jew and Gentile, slaves and free, adults and children, married and single, widowed and divorced, sinners and saints, extroverts and introverts, farmers, priests, kings, queens, carpenters, tentmakers, tax collectors, shepherds, fishermen, religious leaders, homemakers, poets, prophets, preachers, writers, singers, musicians, artists, and many more.

Don't count yourself out of God's plan either. Maybe you feel exceptionally average, but that's not how God sees you. He sees your uniqueness. He knows the grace and gifts he has given you. He cares about the people in need around you. It doesn't matter what your background is, what your skills are, how much education you have, what's in your bank account, or what your Enneagram type is. God has a dream for you. Lots of dreams, in fact.

And if God can still dream for you, you'd better believe you can dream for yourself.

Here Comes That Dreamer

Dreamers are near to God's heart. Just because a few of your dreams have turned out to be nightmares doesn't mean you should stop dreaming. So what if some of your dreams were a little off course or self-focused and God had to adjust them? That doesn't mean you should never plan or imagine again. Or if someone criticized your dream or told you to "be realistic" or "get your head out of the clouds," does that mean you have to listen to the haters?

Read the story of Joseph when you have a chance. It takes up eleven chapters in the Bible (Genesis 37–47), which is a lot of airtime for one guy. I'll summarize the story and then make a few points about dreams, especially broken ones.

The story begins with a dream (a literal one) that Joseph had about his brothers and parents: he saw them bowing down to him. He told his brothers about the dream, which in retrospect probably wasn't a great idea. They were already jealous of him, and this dream made them hate him even more. They saw their chance to end his dreams permanently when he went to check on them while they were working in the fields.

"'Here comes that dreamer!' they said to each other. 'Come now, let's kill him and throw him into one of these cisterns and say that a ferocious animal devoured him. Then we'll see what comes of his dreams'" (Genesis 37:19–20).

"Dreamer" was meant as an insult, but it turned out to be his gift. We'll get to that. As far as the haters' snide little comment, "We'll see what comes of his dreams"—well, they would see, actually. And it wouldn't be what they expected.

Fortunately, they didn't kill him. Unfortunately, though, they sold him as a slave. With brothers like that, who needs enemies? He ended up being trafficked to Egypt, hundreds of miles from home.

Joseph was such a good worker that eventually his master promoted him over his entire estate. Things were looking up—until everything came crashing down. Joseph was falsely accused of attempted rape by his master's wife and ended up in prison. Even in prison he began to find favor and success with the head of the prison. One day he interpreted the dreams of some fellow prisoners—and to everyone's surprise, his interpretations came true, down to the letter. But Joseph was still rotting in jail.

Sometime later Pharaoh had a nightmare that scared him half to death, and he wanted someone to explain what it meant. The ex-prisoner from earlier in the story spoke up: "I know a guy who can interpret dreams." When Pharaoh called for Joseph and told him the dream, Joseph nailed it. He explained the dream's meaning so accurately that Pharaoh promoted him to second-in-command in all of Egypt.

To make a long story short, the dream had to do with a famine that was coming. Joseph wisely made preparations for that famine, so when it happened, Egypt had plenty of food stored up. This is when the brothers entered the story again. They went to Egypt to buy food so they wouldn't die of hunger. They went before the person in charge and bowed down to him. That person, of course, turned out to be Joseph. His original dream had come true. Eventually Joseph was reunited with his family, and they all moved to Egypt where Joseph gave them land and food.

Remember when his brothers sneered about "that dreamer" and then said, "We'll see what comes of his dreams"? Well, they saw all right. They saw Joseph in front of a nation, with unfathomable wealth and power—not for his own glory but to save lives.

Dreamers gonna dream, and haters gonna hate. Let's choose to be the dreamers. The haters will realize their mistakes soon enough.

How to Deal with Broken Dreams

Hopefully you don't have homicidal brothers who resent your dreams and take it upon themselves to sabotage them by selling you into slavery. If you do, get help. That's not normal.

But there's a good chance that you know what it's like to face so much resistance to a dream that you almost *think* you're the victim of a conspiracy. Maybe people have opposed you, or you've made some major mistakes, or circumstances seem to resist you at every turn.

How should you respond?

If it's the wrong dream, let it go.

Let's be honest: not every plan or purpose in our hearts should come to pass. Sometimes what we're imagining is simply wrong. It could be that it's selfish, misguided, impossible, harmful, too far outside our wheelhouse, or not even what we want in the first place.

If you've ever had a wannabe love interest shoot their shot and tell you they're convinced "you are the one" for them, but you are 100 percent certain you are not, then you know that not all dreams should come to pass. Specifically, their dream involving your future wedding.

Yes, we should dream, but let's hold those dreams in open hands. They might need to be surrendered in order to pursue better dreams. Author James Baldwin wrote, "It is only when a man is able, without bitterness or self-pity, to surrender a dream he has long cherished or a privilege he has long possessed that he is set free—he has set himself free—for higher dreams, for greater privileges."[1]

Don't find your security or confidence in the dream.

Your dream should never be the thing you attach your ego or self-worth to. Some people make their job, their fame, or some other goal their entire universe. They believe that achieving that dream will bring them true satisfaction. So they chase mirages forever, never quite laying hold of the permanent peace they thought was just ahead.

No amount of goal reaching can fix a broken soul. Success can bring temporary joy, of course, but it can't make you secure if you were insecure before. It can't make you happy if you were unhappy before. It can't give you peace if you didn't have peace before.

Once we find our security and confidence in God rather than some temporary achievement or accolade, we will be able to pursue our dreams without losing ourselves in the process.

Remember that your dream might have to die before it lives.

Sure, Joseph had his happily ever after, but he had to go through several death experiences to get there, including betrayal, slavery, years of hard work, and years in prison. I'm sure there were times he thought his life was over and all hope was lost. But when the time was right, God fulfilled his dream in ways that were far bigger than Joseph could have imagined. God's dreams are always bigger than human dreams.

Sometimes our dreams have to die, at least temporarily, so that we can die to our dreams. That is, we have to take our ideas and our self-reliance off the pedestal and put them on the altar. Sometimes the death of our little dreams makes way for the realization of God's big dream. Our *good* dream must die to make room for the *best* dream, for a God-sized dream.

When it comes to dreams, timing is everything. Faith and hope rarely operate on our schedule. Many dreams take years to be fulfilled, and even then, it's often in stages, a little bit at a time. Don't have such a specific idea of how and when your dream will be fulfilled that you miss it when it happens. And don't assume that just because you haven't seen any progress in a while, the dream is dead. Joseph's life changed overnight, and so can yours.

Let God bring good out of evil.

Joseph's brothers were understandably afraid of him once they realized who he was. They thought he would get revenge by killing them. Instead, he said these amazing words: "You intended to harm me, but God intended it for good to accomplish what is now being done, the saving of many lives" (Genesis 50:20).

Joseph understood something that we need to grasp too: God's dreams are much bigger than ours, and sometimes the enemies, obstacles, or detours we face are moving us forward on our journeys. The difficulties are confusing now, even painful, but someday things will make more sense. We'll realize that a lot of what we resented was actually working for good. As Paul wrote to the Romans, "In all things God works for the good of those who love him, who have been called according to his purpose" (8:28).

Dream bigger than you.

How do you know if your dream is too small? If it benefits only you. God's dreams are big dreams because they include the world. When Joseph first dreamed, he saw his family bowing to him. He must have imagined wealth, authority, and fame. When they actually did bow to him many years later, the point wasn't Joseph's clout: it was the fact that he was using what he had been given to serve others.

God's dreams for you include you, but they are bigger than you. His blessings are meant to be spread far and wide. I'm talking about generosity. About love. About empathy. About allyship. About unity. About empowerment. Those are the kinds of dreams God likes to get behind, and those are the dreams that bring the deepest fulfillment.

Follow the Giver of Dreams

I wish I could say Patty Shakes was the only dream of mine that never came true, but that would be far from the truth. I've experienced many other broken dreams, and I'm sure there will be others ahead. I'm okay with that. I'd rather have a few dreams not come true than never dream at all.

The reality is that some dreams are simply not meant to be. We need to settle in our hearts that as finite humans, it's unrealistic and unhealthy to think we can foresee everything about the future. We have to go into the dreaming process knowing that some things will work out as we expect, but many won't. Some will turn out worse and some will turn out better. Either way, God is still on the throne, he's still sovereign, and he's still on our side.

Broken dreams remind us of some important truths, though: We don't place our hope in dreams. We don't attach our egos to success. We don't define our worth by the goals we reach. Or at least we *shouldn't* do any of those things. Dreams are wonderful, but they don't have power to bring soul-level satisfaction. And they cannot compare to the original and ultimate dreamer, God himself.

Are you dealing with discouragement and pain over a dream that never came true? If so, take advantage of the moment to draw closer to God. Give your expectations to him. Let him hang on to your dream for a while. You are safe in his arms, and your dream is safe in his hands.

At the same time don't be in a hurry to write it off. Maybe the dream is dead, or maybe *your version* of the dream is dead. It's possible God still intends to bring it to pass, but in his way, his time, and his strength. If that's the case, he probably wants to polish and expand and fine-tune the dream a little. He'll likely want to tweak a few things inside of you too. And he'll take the time he needs to put things in place that are outside your view.

All of that is up to him. So what do you do? Stay close to the Dreamer. Learn his ways, listen to his voice—and keep dreaming.

NINE

When the Ground Shakes: Losing Security

The Fukushima nuclear disaster in March 2011 was one of the worst nuclear power plant incidents ever. That event is etched into my mind, partly because it seemed to come out of nowhere. Nuclear reactors are some of the most carefully controlled places in the world, after all. They have contingency plans for their contingency plans.

The disaster didn't originate in the reactor, though. It started off the coast of Japan, deep under the ocean, with a magnitude-9.0 earthquake that lasted for six minutes. This caused the reactors' energy supply to fail, meaning the reactor could no longer cool itself down.

There were emergency generators for just that sort of thing, though, so the problem was under control. Except it wasn't. The earthquake caused a forty-nine-foot-high tsunami that swept over the seawall and shut down the emergency pumps. From there everything spiraled out of control, leading to multiple nuclear meltdowns and explosions.[1]

It was a massive disaster, and it started because ground that should have been as solid as a rock turned into Jell-O, and water that should have stayed in the ocean became an aquatic mountain that rolled across dry land.

Have you ever been in an earthquake? They are terrifying. Even small ones. First of all, random objects can come crashing down on your head, which for obvious reasons is not a good thing. But on a more fundamental level, earthquakes are scary because the one thing that seems most permanent and trustworthy in this world—solid ground—proves to be as unstable as water. You find yourself betrayed by something you never thought to doubt.

What to Do When the Shaking Starts

This feeling of panic, even betrayal, isn't limited to physical earthquakes, of course. When our mental, emotional, or financial worlds are hit by a magnitude-9.0 quake and things we assumed were solid and secure start crashing down on our heads, the same panic sets in. The same fear. The same sense of loss and confusion. When the things we believed to be untouchable, unshakable, and unmovable start rocking and rolling around us, it makes us question what—if anything—is trustworthy. What sources of our security can be shaken? Is anything safe if solid ground can turn to water under our feet?

Any significant loss of security can feel like a form of death. Maybe you lost an investment you had been planning to retire on, and now you are mourning the death of your financial stability. Maybe your church went through a scandal or division, and you are grieving the loss of your spiritual community. Maybe your body isn't responding like it used to, and you are struggling to adjust to your reduced physical capabilities. These are "little deaths" that affect your sense of security, and they need to be recognized and addressed just as much as any other loss.

The most obvious place where we might experience loss of security is our income. For example, what would happen if the company you worked for went bankrupt, or you were fired unexpectedly, or you were unable to work due to illness or injury? If your spouse is the main breadwinner, what would happen to your family if they lost their job? If you are a business owner and one of your biggest clients dropped you or your competition took over most of the market share, how would you recover? Or if you had a family tragedy and were unable to work, how would your bills get paid? Steady income is great when you have it, but when it suddenly disappears, you realize how fragile the ground was that you were standing on.

Money is a big source of security, but it's not the only one. Another is *family*. Maybe as a child you experienced the divorce of your parents. Your world was your home and family, and suddenly that world fractured. Two homes, two lives, two directions. And you were caught in the middle. Or maybe you didn't lose your parents to divorce, but you lost a loved one to a tragic death, or your own marriage fell apart, or a child cut off contact with you and refuses to be reconciled.

You can probably think of other sources of security. *Routine* is secure and comforting, at least for many people. *Religion, faith,* and a *church community* certainly create stability too. The *home, city,* and *country* you live in, the *friend group* you belong to, your *physical and mental abilities*, and much more contribute to a sense of security we often take for grante=d.

All those things can be shaken. That's what is so scary. Just like the not-so-solid ground we walk on, work on, and build houses on, every "secure" foundation this planet has to offer can move when we least expect it. And when it does, everything can come tumbling down.

You've probably experienced something like this in your life. I know I have. Out of the blue, you get some bad news, and your world feels like it's falling apart around you. You don't even know how to process what you just learned. What's next? How will you recover? How will you live? How will you feed your family?

It is incredibly disconcerting to lose what you thought was solid ground. Whether that is your life savings, your career, a parent, your home, or a pet, you can be left feeling confused and even terrified.

By the way, sources of security are not always as external as those I just listed. Often they are internal: your faith, your concept of God, your perception of your own goodness, your self-esteem, your patriotism or view of your country, your political affiliation, your biases, your logic, your experiences, and so on. All of these combine to create a worldview that works for you—more or less, anyway—and that gives you security. You might not be able to control the world, but at least you can fit it into your worldview.

But what happens when someone or something undermines part of that worldview? It can feel like everything is threatened. We're going to talk more about that later on, because often our biggest resistance to change is the emotional panic we feel when our belief system is challenged. For now, though, just be aware that our need for stability is a powerful thing. Learn to question your reactions. Things that cause you to feel uncertain and unsettled might not be wrong; maybe they are just scary because they are rocking something you assumed was settled.

Whether internal or external, a loss of security is a death experience. It might not be as easily defined as the loss of relationships or dreams, which we looked at in the last two chapters, but it's just as real. That's why anxiety and grief are such common feelings when we lose something we were counting on. Our sources of security are dead, and we are at a crossroads. We can no longer count on those things to give us hope or stability.

Here's the thing, though: everything that can be shaken will be shaken. We need to get used to shaking. We need to expect it. And we even need to appreciate it.

Rather than letting the earthquakes of the soul send us running in panic, we must look around and see how wobbly and flimsy some of our assumptions really are. The shaking helps us see what is stable and what is not. The shaking reminds us not to put our trust in the wrong things. The shaking points us back to God, the only unshakable foundation in the entire universe. The prophet Isaiah said this:

> "Though the mountains be shaken
> and the hills be removed,
> yet my unfailing love for you will not be shaken
> nor my covenant of peace be removed,"
> says the LORD, who has compassion on you.
>
> (54:10)

David wrote something similar: "I keep my eyes always on the LORD. With him at my right hand, I will not be shaken" (Psalm 16:8).

In the face of shaking, both Isaiah and David recommended the same thing: look up. God cannot be shaken, of course. His love is unfailing, his compassion is built into his nature, and his promise of peace is a rock-solid guarantee.

God cannot be shaken, so you will not be shaken.

No matter what shakes around us, God is still on the throne. And he's not even spilling his coffee, because earthquakes can't move heaven. They are, by definition, limited to the earth.

When everything in your world is shaking, put your trust in the one who transcends the world. The one who walks on water. The one who stills the wind and the waves, who set the stars in motion and knows them all by name, who has counted every hair on your head, who knows more about you and cares more about you than you do.

God cannot be shaken, so you will not be shaken.

Be Shook but Not Shaken

Here's a question worth asking: What did David mean when he wrote, "I will not be shaken"?

If you read the story of his life in the Bible, it's pretty clear that he did not mean that life would be easy and comfortable and fun all the time. Remember, David is the guy who faced a giant with a slingshot. He spent years hiding in deserts and caves from a manic-depressive, homicidal king who wanted his head. David's family was even kidnapped by an enemy tribe. As king he made some really big mistakes in his personal life, including, but not limited to, adultery and murder. And to top it off, he was plotted against and nearly assassinated by his own son.

David faced a lot of tough times. Pretty much every source of security he had was taken away at one point or another, and I'm sure those moments felt like a kind of death. So how could he say, "I will not be shaken"? Because he was referring to his *soul*. He was saying that on the inside he was strong. His faith was solid, his inner peace was secure, his relationship with God was unmovable. Though he was surrounded by death (both literally and figuratively), his source of security was higher than any of those things. The loss of temporary, earthly, superficial sources of security only reminded him to place his trust in something higher than that, on a "rock that is higher than I," as he put it (Psalm 61:2).

David was not saying that he was some emotionless stone statue, though. Just read the Psalms. He spent a lot of time crying, venting, questioning, and complaining. His emotions and feelings and thoughts were shaking all the time. There's an old James Brown breakup song called "I'm Shook." The entire chorus consists of the lines "I'm all shook up," and "I said I'm shook."[2] David could have related to that song. He spent a lot of time shook: dumbfounded, astonished, confused, scared, shocked, speechless, sad.

There's a difference between being shaken and being shook, though. David's emotions were all over the place, but ultimately his security was in God. His declaration that "I will not be shaken" referred to his inner sense of security in God. He was saying that deep down, he knew he would be okay.

In other words, he was shook but not shaken. He had peace in God, and that peace was projected into his external world.

The kidnapping of his family is a perfect example of this. The story is found in 1 Samuel 30. David was in exile, hiding from the current king (Saul) who wanted to kill him out of jealousy. David had an army of misfits who had joined him, and they were constantly in danger from Saul, from roving tribes of marauders, and from neighboring armies. It was not an easy life for those who had chosen to stand with David.

One day while David and his men were away dealing with one enemy, another enemy group swept through the town where they were based and took everything precious to them: their wives, their children, and all their possessions. When the army returned to camp and found everything gone, David's men were so heartbroken and angry that they talked of killing David.

How did David respond? "David was greatly distressed because the men were talking of stoning him; each one was bitter in spirit because of his sons and daughters. But David found strength in the LORD his God" (1 Samuel 30:6).

Did you catch that last phrase? He found his *strength* in his *God*.

I wish I could see that video. Did he pray? Cry? Yell? Sing? Sit in silence? Probably all the above, and more. Somehow he tapped into the unshakable presence of God within him. He renewed his strength and his faith. He found his courage again.

Then he took action. He sought God's direction for his next step, which is always a wise move. Then he led his army to a resounding victory and they recovered everything.

What would have happened if David had allowed the shaking on the outside to shatter him on the inside? What if he had given up on God? On himself? On his men and their families? Somehow David was able to look past the uncertainty and insecurity of temporal things and see that truly, in God, he would not be shaken.

The same goes for us. The shaking on the outside doesn't have to shake us on the inside. When the world falls around us, it doesn't mean our world has to fall within us. We can turn to God and find strength.

Strength in God is more permanent than possessions, more valuable than money, and more trustworthy than anything this world has to offer. Strength in God can chase down the enemy and reclaim what was stolen. It can rebuild what was burned to ashes. It can mourn for what was lost, then stand to its feet and believe for the future.

The apostle Paul, like David, had an unshakable faith. He wrote, "But we have this treasure in jars of clay to show that this all-surpassing power is from God and not from us. We are hard pressed on every side, but not crushed; perplexed, but not in despair; persecuted, but not abandoned; struck down, but not destroyed" (2 Corinthians 4:7–9).

It is precisely the shaking that reveals the treasure. And that treasure is God himself. His strength, his presence, and his mercy are unbreakable and unstoppable.

Maybe you're shook right now. Maybe you feel like the ground won't stop moving beneath you. You lost something important, something that used to give you security. The fear and grief you feel are part of the process, because you aren't just letting a source of security die; you are dying to that source of security.

If you're wondering whether you'll ever feel safe again . . . you will.

Because you *are* safe. Right now you are safe in God's arms. Let the shaking do what shaking does best: reveal the frailty of human hope and the reality of God's presence.

Then find your safety, security, and stability in the unshakable love of God.

TEN

Spinning Out and Letting Go: Losing Control

About two years after I started driving, we had a bad snowstorm in North Carolina. That amount of snowfall was not a common occurrence where we lived. Our local government didn't have the infrastructure to handle it, so the wet snow sat on the ground for four days until a lot of it turned into black ice.

Black ice is not actually black, of course. It's transparent. Instead of being white and obvious like normal ice, it blends into the road so you can't see it. All you know is that one moment you are driving and the next moment you are ice-skating, and your pedals and steering wheel are totally useless.

I didn't really know any of that back then, though. One day I had to run an errand, and my parents had told me that if I was going to drive anywhere, I had to be cautious, drive slowly, and pay attention. Naturally at that age I thought two years of driving made me a total expert, and I couldn't imagine losing control of my vehicle. I'd never encountered winter weather like this, and black ice was not even on my radar.

As I started off on my errand, it immediately became obvious that this was going to be trickier than I had expected. Less than five minutes down the road, I came to a steep hill. I attempted to drive up the hill and got exactly nowhere. The wheels were spinning at top speed, but the car wasn't going anywhere. Well, it was sliding sideways, but that didn't really count.

I thought I was in control, at least at first. But that illusion was shattered when my car finally spun out of control, off the road, and onto an embankment of dirt and mud. I sat there for a moment trying to regain my composure and my pride. Then with two wheels on the dirt and two wheels on the street, I inched my way up the hill and back home.

So much for being in control. I've had a healthy respect for snow and ice ever since that day.

Driving in snowstorms isn't the only time we feel out of control, of course. I'm sure we all feel this way quite often. This brings up the next issue we need to consider: *control*. Or more accurately, the *illusion* of control. Or even more accurately, the *loss* of the illusion of control. Because that's when things really fall apart, right? When the fragile grip we had on our world proves to be even weaker than we thought, and we're left staring at the lifeless remains of our self-reliance.

A lot of people have a tough time when things start spinning out of control. They feel anxiety, stress, anger, and grief. These people do their best to restore order, to keep all the balls in the air—but all too often, it's a losing battle, and the result is not pretty.

It's me. I'm people.

And you probably are too.

You're Not in Control Anyway

Now, control is not a bad thing. Not at all. Control is usually a *good* thing. If your emotions are out of control, you hurt people. If your finances are out of control, you run out of money. If your sexual desires or your drinking habits are out of control, you do all kinds of things you regret later. We are hardwired as humans to stay in control, because the alternative—being out of control—rarely ends well.

We learn from a young age to get control and keep control. We learn to manipulate our environment and leverage our influence to our advantage. Again, this is not wrong. The Bible has a lot to say about controlling our tongues, our money, our desires, and our actions. This is called *self-control*, and it's considered a virtue by practically every society. For example, Proverbs says, "Better a patient person than a warrior, one with self-control than one who takes a city" (16:32). Later in the same book, we read, "Like a city whose walls are broken through is a person who lacks self-control" (25:28). Self-control even makes it onto Paul's "fruit of the Spirit" list in Galatians 5:22–23.

Yet there's a difference between self-control and everything-control. God gives us grace to do the first but not the second. When we try to control things outside of our spheres, we set ourselves up for failure. And eventually, a funeral.

That's why people often refer to the "illusion of control." You might have your life planned out a year in advance. You might think your finances are recession-proof. You might know where your kids are every minute of every day. You might eat vegan and exercise religiously and take enough pills to stock a pharmacy.

But that doesn't guarantee anything. The calendar, the economy, your kids, and your health are influenced by a lot of factors beyond your control. Control is an illusion. As Ecclesiastes reminds us,

> The race is not to the swift
> or the battle to the strong,
> nor does food come to the wise

or wealth to the brilliant
or favor to the learned;
but time and chance happen to them all.

(9:11)

Can you increase the likelihood of success with good planning and hard work? Yes! Should you do your best to have your life in order? Of course! Literally one verse earlier, we read, "Whatever your hand finds to do, do it with all your might" (v. 10). God has given us free will and a lot of resources, and he certainly wants us to use them wisely.

Just remember there will be times when you have to say goodbye to control. And that's going to hurt. It might even feel a little like death.

Why is it so hard to relinquish control? Because just as with the other areas we've looked at, you're really dying to *yourself*. You're coming face-to-face with your limitations, your humanity, your weakness.

That's about as much fun as a funeral. And in a sense, it *is* a funeral. A funeral for the ego. A funeral for arrogance. A funeral for selfishness. A funeral for fear. These are all things that can motivate our thirst for control.

My goal isn't to call us all control freaks or overanalyze motivations that we probably can't fully understand. Instead, it's to point out that burying our need for control is one of the most liberating things we can do.

Too often we buy into the fallacy that the more control we have over our environment or the future, the less risk we will have, so the more freedom we will experience. That's only true to a point, though. Eventually the very things you think will give you more control end up exposing you to more risk. That's the irony of growth.

For example, more money means more freedom—but it also

means more worries about how to protect your money, how to make more of it, how to manage your employees and keep your clients, how to pay your creditors, and how to keep up with the lifestyle wealth has bought you. So more money also brings more risk.

Similarly, more authority means more freedom—but it also means more responsibility, more demands, more decisions, more complaints, more vulnerability, more delegation, and more people to care for. Again, that means more risk.

All I'm pointing out here is that control cannot eliminate risk. Do you want to live without fear of loss? The answer is not to control everyone and everything all the time. Not only is that impossible, but ultimately it will only make losses worse.

Instead, you have to learn to *let go.*

I'm not saying let go of self-control, nor am I saying let go of the things you're reasonably expected to control. I'm saying let go of your tendency toward everything-control. It's killing you anyway. And it's probably driving those around you bats.

One of my favorite Scripture verses is Proverbs 16:9. "In their hearts humans plan their course, but the LORD establishes their steps." So go ahead and make plans. Plans are good. Plans are helpful. Plans are smart. But plans don't have the final say—only God does. You can give God control and trust him to do what's best.

How to Let Go Without Giving Up

So what does it mean to let go? And how is letting go different from giving up? Here are a few ideas to get you started:

1. To let go is to become a learner.

    Pride is often at the root of control because we think we know best. Humility, on the other hand, is willing to learn.

There is so much freedom in becoming a learner. You don't have to know everything, explain everything, or project-manage everything. Once your ego is out of the way, you are free to listen and learn.

2. To let go is to allow for risk.

Racing legend Mario Andretti famously said, "If everything seems under control, you're just not going fast enough."[1] Don't try to eliminate risk by increasing control beyond what is right. Instead, get used to risk. That's called *risk tolerance*. Life is more fun when you're not terrified of failing but instead embrace mistakes as a normal part of the growth process.

3. To let go is to recover awe.

There is something awe-inspiring about being under the Milky Way on a pitch-black night, or standing on the beach at sunset watching waves painted purple and gold, or hiking in the mountains when summer is merging with autumn and the leaves are changing colors. It's a feeling of smallness that is good for the soul. You realize the universe is a lot bigger than you give it credit for, and you are a lot smaller. You might think that would be scary, but it's comforting. You don't have to be God. Instead, you get to be human. That's a gift.

4. To let go is to be okay with your humanity.

Think about how fragile humans are. We can't fly, or see in the dark, or breathe underwater. We bruise and break. We age. We have to sleep every night. We get hungry multiple times a day. And yet we are God's delight, made in his image, chosen to reflect him, to be with him, to be loved by him. Letting go of our need for absolute control is found at the intersection of those two truths: we are small, but we are infinitely valuable.

5. To let go is to rely on other people.

One of the greatest truths we discover when we lose control is that we don't have to do life alone. Funerals are always full of people: concerned friends and family who gather around the bereaved to comfort them, console them, and stuff them with as much food as possible. When everything is going perfectly, we often think we are fine on our own. But in the face of tragedy or loss that strips us of control, we realize the greatest gift is people.

6. To let go is to bounce back quickly.

Letting go of control includes letting go of the self-imposed shame of failure. Think about basketball for a moment. Even the greatest players miss easy shots sometimes. That's embarrassing, sure—but the game isn't going to stop so they can have the luxury of a pity party, temper tantrum, or guilt trip. They have to shake off the mistake, get their heads in the right space, and keep playing the game. I'm not saying that in times of failure or tragedy, genuine sorrow or other emotions should just be shaken off. But shame should be. Petty temper tantrums and pity parties and guilt trips should be. If they aren't helping you get back in the right headspace so you can win the game, let them go.

7. To let go is to trust God in the good and the bad.

Finally, and most importantly, letting go means letting God be God, no matter what. I'm not talking about some fatalistic approach to life where you never try to do anything or improve anything because "everything happens for a reason." I'm talking about doing your absolute best while recognizing that all the things outside your control are still within the realm of God's sovereignty. Maybe your expectations weren't met, but that doesn't mean God failed. You just need to adjust your expectations.

The Whole World in His Hands

Often what keeps us bound to the illusion of control is the assumption that if we don't watch out for ourselves, nobody will. That's false, though. Just because we are not in control doesn't mean no one is in control. God is still there, watching and loving and guiding us forward.

If you grew up in church, you might remember singing an old Sunday school song that goes, "He's got the whole world in his hands." The song was essentially infinite because you could replace "whole world" with just about anything. Sometimes we'd sing that song for twenty minutes straight. "He's got you and me in his hands . . . He's got mom and dad in his hands . . . He's got the little bitty baby in his hands . . ." You get the picture.

> You go to sleep every night, and the world doesn't fall apart.

You might want to sing this chorus to yourself and update the words to fit your current scenario. Perhaps something like, "He's got my mostly empty bank account in his hands . . . He's got my cranky neighbor in his hands . . . He's got the upcoming elections in his hands . . ." It's a good reminder that his hands are a lot bigger than yours.

Remember, you go to sleep every night, and the world doesn't fall apart. The earth keeps orbiting the sun. Your heart keeps beating, and your chest keeps filling with air. Your brain happily chugs along, and all your bodily systems work without your conscious control. You have zero control and absolute peace, all at the same time.

What if, when you woke up tomorrow morning, you tried to keep that same peace throughout the day? You are not in control of most of your existence, and that's a good thing. Let go of the pressure to maintain the illusion of self-sufficiency. You're not fooling anyone anyway. Besides, God's got this.

ELEVEN

New Sheriff in Town: Losing Sin

As I've grown older I've noticed some changes happening in my body. It used to be that no matter what I ate, how much I rested, or what I did all day, I could go to sleep just fine at night and wake up the next morning feeling like new. My body could handle pretty much anything I threw at it and act as if nothing had happened.

Not anymore.

Recently my body has started talking back to me. It has developed a bit of an attitude, and I can't get away with the things I used to. For example, this year I ruptured my Achilles tendon on my left foot while playing basketball. I had to have surgery, then I spent about a month and a half with a cast on. That meant I was pretty much stuck on the couch for six straight weeks, and I was no longer able to exercise, work out, or play sports.

One thing I have always thoroughly enjoyed is good milk chocolate, and whenever I had a craving for it, I'd eat a piece or two with no real effect on my body. However, while I was glued to the couch recovering from my Achilles injury, that infrequent guilty pleasure turned into a daily habit. In my mind I wasn't consuming that much chocolate—but the *frequency* meant I was consuming a lot more calories than I realized. And my body quickly showed the results.

Once I got the cast off my foot (and my rear end off the couch), I thought I could bounce back quickly. But as it turns out, I couldn't. My body is not as forgiving in my forties as it used to be, which meant I had to make the difficult choice to totally eliminate chocolate from my diet for an extended period of time. That felt a little bit like death. Death by dieting.

You can probably relate. Maybe it wasn't chocolate you had to give up but rather a television habit, or social media, or drinking, or any one of a million things that we think are good at first but ultimately turn out to hurt us. While I'm joking (sort of) about the emotional impact of giving up chocolate, these self-imposed sacrifices are not easy. Often we can feel like a small part of us has been put to death.

So far we've talked about losing people, dreams, security, and control. These are all things that typically are *taken from you*. You walk through pain or loss because it's forced upon you, not because you chose it. You hold a metaphorical funeral to commemorate a death experience you didn't want or maybe even expect. Now, though, I'd like to look at things you *give up voluntarily*. Rather than being a death inflicted on you, it's one you choose to go through. It's a funeral you initiate. Why would you do that? Because the thing you need to bury is actually killing you. It needs to be removed from your life before it causes you greater damage.

This is about much more than milk chocolate, of course. In reality I'm talking primarily about the things the Bible would call *sin*. Not just the external sins that get most of the airtime—lying, cheating, stealing, immorality, yelling at bad drivers on the freeway, or rooting for the Falcons or Buccaneers. We also need to consider the internal sins: the issues we hide from everyone (including from ourselves, more often than not), such as greed, fear, anger, and pride. These are the things that lie at the root of the external problems we usually focus on. And until we die to them, they'll keep killing us.

Let me give you some examples. Maybe you have an anger issue that you've tried to keep under control, but now it's affecting your family. Maybe you have a drinking problem that you told yourself was a minor issue, but now it's damaging your health. Maybe you've done some shady business deals or made decisions that lacked integrity, and now those things are coming back to haunt you.

Sooner or later sin has a way of surfacing, and often at the worst possible time. When it does, and when you see the damage and pain it causes, you're going to want to change. There comes a moment when you realize you have to deal with whatever weakness, addiction, or temptation you have, because it's not getting any better. It's not going away on its own. And if left unchecked, it's going to have some pretty damaging effects on your life.

It's like one of the old Westerns where an outlaw and a sheriff face off in the middle of the street at high noon. "This town ain't big enough for the both of us," somebody usually mutters. Townspeople rush their kids indoors and shutter their windows. Cliché music plays in the background. Suddenly guns are drawn. Dust flies. The volume of the cliché music intensifies. When the dust clears, only one person is left standing—hopefully the good guy.

Either you face your issues and come out victorious, or you run away and hide.

The good guy is you, FYI. This is a duel to the death between your inner self and this intruder, this outlaw, who is trying to undermine the person you want to be. Either you face your issues and come out victorious, or you run away and hide. This town ain't big enough for the both of you.

Don't Be the One Who Holds You Back

So who are the "outlaws" you might face? What are the root issues, the wrong desires, the toxic tendencies that you need to bury?

Ultimately you have to figure that out for yourself. These are *your* most wanted outlaws, your inner demons, and nobody knows them like you. However, if you need help, try asking your friends and family. They'll have some opinions on the subject, I'm sure. And they might even be right.

Most of the time the issues we face are the same ones the human race has been struggling with since the beginning. Remember Adam and Eve? Their greed, self-will, and pride led them to break the one command God had given them, opening the door for death and sin to enter history. Cain and Abel are another example. Cain's envy, anger, and hatred are what fueled the first murder. Though today we wear more clothes than Adam and Eve, and we don't offer up fruit and animal sacrifices like Cain and Abel, we can totally relate to them. We've faced the same temptations, felt the same urges, acted from the same motivations. There haven't been any new sins invented in the thousands of years since our ancestors first tried to figure out what it meant to be human. There are a lot of new *ways* to sin, for sure, but the root issues are unchanged.

That's why the Bible continues to be relevant. It must be interpreted in light of the culture it was written in, of course, but the heart issues it speaks to are the exact same as the ones we experience today. So are the advice, encouragement, and wisdom it teaches. We can find help in the pages of Scripture because we find *ourselves* in those pages.

Teachers, preachers, and religious leaders throughout history have tried to list the main temptations or sins people face. Some of the early Christian writers summarized them in seven "capital sins," as they are often called (or deadly, or cardinal). In theory these are the basic sins, the foundational ones from which all the others spring. Traditionally they include pride, greed, lust, envy, gluttony, anger, and laziness.

I'm not sure how gluttony made the list. I feel like there are other sins that outrank gluttony in terms of harm. What exactly constitutes gluttony, anyway? Is there a calorie limit? A specific number of pizza slices that crosses the line?

Laziness also makes me wonder. How late can you sleep in on Saturday before it becomes a capital sin? Are morning people closer to godliness than night owls? Does God get mad when we hit the Snooze button multiple times?

I'm kidding, of course. All of these categories of sin are human-defined and maddeningly relative. They are invisible and immeasurable, issues of the heart and mind and will. Again, that's why only you can ultimately determine what constitutes an enemy. Some things just need to be tweaked a little. Others need to be challenged to a duel, shot dead in the street, and buried on a hill outside of town. If that sounds violent, it's because it is. This is a fight. A life-or-death struggle against things that will harm us and those around us if we give in to them.

The common denominator among all the internal enemies we face is *a focus on self*. Ultimately that's what sin is: a willingness to put selfish desires and pursuits above everything and everyone, including God.

That means the funeral we need to attend is our own. We need to die to *ourselves*. Or more accurately, to our *self*. We need to die to our egos, our selfish desires, our unchecked needs, our independence.

I'm not saying that our desires and needs don't matter but rather that we can't make them our one and only pursuit in life. We exist within a much wider context where family, friends, classmates, co-workers, and even strangers also have desires and needs. When we elevate our wants and needs beyond what is right, and when we forget or ignore those around us, we create a monster. A monster called *self*. A monster who needs to die.

Remember what Jesus told his disciples? "Whoever wants to be my disciple must deny themselves and take up their cross and follow me. For whoever wants to save their life will lose it, but whoever loses their life for me and for the gospel will save it. What good is it for someone to gain the whole world, yet forfeit their soul? Or what can anyone give in exchange for their soul?" (Mark 8:34–37).

Jesus was saying that if we really want to be like him, we're going to have to deactivate the selfishness that comes factory-installed in the human soul. That's not a one-time thing but rather a lifestyle of self-control that is motivated by love and directed by wisdom.

Underlying all the issues you must overcome is a hyperfocus on self. On *you*. That means if you are going to deal with these issues, you're going to be dealing with you. And you will tend to fight back.

The Bible says that we are to offer ourselves to God as living sacrifices (Romans 12:1). I heard someone say that the problem with living sacrifices is they tend to get up off the altar. I know that's true of me. Probably you too.

Dying to yourself hurts. There's a price to pay. There's a cost to this. If you aren't willing to say no to yourself, you'll never overcome what is holding you back, because *you* are what is holding you back. Paul put it this way:

Put to death, therefore, whatever belongs to your earthly nature: sexual immorality, impurity, lust, evil desires and greed, which is idolatry. Because of these, the wrath of God is coming. You used to walk in these ways, in the life you once lived. But now you must also rid yourselves of all such things as these: anger, rage, malice, slander, and filthy language from your lips. Do not lie to each other, since you have taken off your old self with its practices and have put on the new self, which is being renewed in knowledge in the image of its Creator. (Colossians 3:5–10)

The good news is that putting to death the old self allows us to bring to life the new self. There is no new life without death, as we saw earlier. When we die to our old selves, to the sin and selfishness that used to define us, we become alive to God. That new life is far better than what we left behind. It's a life characterized by grace, love, joy, and peace. A life that embraces and builds and serves others. It's the reality Jesus came to give us: life, and life more abundantly (John 10:10).

Love Is the Answer

Since sin is a fixation with self, *love* is the best antidote to sin. Sin looks out for number one; love looks out for everyone. Sin is willing to sacrifice others for self; love is willing to sacrifice self for others. Sin delights in getting; love delights in giving.

Remember when Jesus was asked what the greatest commandment was? He replied with two things, which feels like cheating, but he's God so he can get away with it. Plus, his answers were two sides of the same coin—a coin called *love*: "'Love the Lord your God with all your heart and with all your soul and with all your mind.' This is the first and greatest commandment. And the second is like it: 'Love your neighbor as yourself.' All the Law and the Prophets hang on these two commandments" (Matthew 22:37–40).

The reason love is the greatest command is because you can't love someone and still be okay with hurting them. Love counteracts sin by undermining its very motivation, which is selfish by nature. Paul wrote, "Love does no harm to a neighbor. Therefore love is the fulfillment of the law" (Romans 13:10).

Regardless of the particular weakness or moral failing you might be struggling with, love will go a long way toward overcoming it. Maybe you're fighting an addiction, a bad habit, a dysfunction, a character flaw, a personality quirk, a chemical dependency, or some other inner demon. While I can't promise you a quick fix, I can tell you that leaning on love is essential.

> Let his love for you give you the confidence to fight your inner battles.

What do I mean by leaning on love? First, accept God's love. Let his love for you give you the confidence to fight your inner battles. He's not mad at you or frustrated with you. He believes in you, and he'll be with you all the way.

Second, let his love flow through you. Make love your compass, your goal, and your measure of success. The selfish nature of sin can't win against the generosity of love. I'm not saying you'll be perfect overnight, but you'll find it a lot easier to see clearly and make healthy choices.

The Top Ten Most Wanted List

Briefly, then, let's think about some of the inner outlaws on our most wanted list. There are more, of course, but these are ones I often encounter, both in me and in people I speak with. If any of these are common problems for you, then it's time to hold a funeral.

1. Pride

    Pride is thinking of yourself more highly than you should, usually in comparison to others (Philippians 2:1–11). It is devastating because it isolates us from anyone who could correct us, including God. It tells us that we are right, we are the best, we are infallible, we are in control, and we don't need anyone else. Check your pride level: Do you need to die to your ego today?

2. Greed

    Greed is about wanting *more* than you should have or about wanting it *sooner* than you should have it. Greed can never make you happy, though. The human capacity for pleasure is a black hole. It's not necessarily wrong to want more money, happiness, comfort, friends, and so on, but if getting more begins to consistently trump loving your neighbor, you've got an outlaw on your hands.

3. Lust

    Lust is often equated with improper sexual desire. It includes that, of course, but it's not limited to it. Lust is any desire that is either *out of control* or *out of context*. Lust is about an appetite that is so voracious it must be satisfied at any cost. It can be a lust for power, fame, comfort, food, money, pleasure, possessions, and more. Addictions could fit under this category as well. Are there areas or appetites you have a tough time controlling? If so, don't hide from the fight.

4. Fear

    I wouldn't call all fear sin, because fear can also be a good emotion that protects and cautions you. However, if fear has expanded to the point that it controls you and hurts you, then it's time to get rid of it. It will steal your joy, your peace, and your opportunities. Think about your fear level. How often do you hide or shrink back? Is fear stealing from you? It might be time to draw a line in the sand.

5. Insecurity

Insecurity is a constant need to prop up your ego and your self-esteem. I'm continually amazed at the power of insecurity to warp our actions and reactions. It's a subtle force that affects everything. Insecure people compete and compare, they put people down to feel better, they react defensively to correction, and they live in constant fear and shame. Insecurity can be hard to identify because it tends to self-protect, so be honest: How are your self-image, self-esteem, and self-confidence doing?

6. Anger and abuse

Anger, like fear, is not always wrong. But when it is uncontrolled, it can go very bad very quickly. It can lead to violence, abuse, broken friendships, and bad health. How often do you lose your temper? How do you act or speak when you get mad? If anger is a problem, get angry with anger. Get mad at immaturity. Use your passion to control yourself, not to lash out at others.

7. Dishonesty

Dishonesty includes things like lying, cheating, manipulation, and deceit. Truth matters. Integrity matters. Your reputation matters. Your word matters. People need to know they can count on you. If your word stops carrying weight, so will your reputation. Think about how often or how easily you lie. Are you willing to pay the price to be a person of integrity?

8. Laziness

By *laziness* I don't mean someone who enjoys naps in the afternoon. I mean someone who just doesn't do the work they need to do. This includes apathy, a poor work ethic, and mediocrity. It might look like showing up late to work or not meeting work obligations. Do you struggle with laziness? Challenge it to a duel. Begin to build a healthy work ethic. Redefine yourself and your approach toward hard things. Your future self will thank you.

9. Jealousy and ungratefulness

Jealousy or envy refers to wanting what someone else has. It includes being discontent with what you have and ungrateful for your blessings. To be jealous is about comparison, and not in a good way (if there is a good way). When a child is jealous of another kid's toy, what do we tell them? Usually to be grateful for what they have, to be happy for the other person, and to work hard so they can buy one of their own. Seems like that advice applies when you're an adult too. How are your contentment level and your gratitude meter doing?

10. Meanness

This might not be a very technical term, but you know what I'm talking about. Some people are just mean. The way they treat other people is hurtful, damaging, and outright wrong. They might be abusive, whether emotionally or physically. They might be violent. They might be bullies. Meanness is more than having a bad day or being in a bad mood. It's a philosophy of how to treat others that looks nothing like Jesus. Take a hard look at how you treat people, especially those close to you. Do you need to root out some meanness from your life?

I'll stop with those ten, but there are more that come to mind. I probably should have included chocolate addiction in there somewhere, but that one still hits too close to home.

How about you? What do you struggle with? What frustrates you? What have loved ones and friends told you that you need to work on? What have bosses (or ex-bosses) had to confront you about? What is making you feel embarrassed or guilty? What is holding you back? What is hurting others around you?

This isn't meant to be an exercise in shame. Not at all. It's about freedom, and it's about taking back ownership of your life. That's the point of holiness, after all—to improve life. It's not about keeping God happy, or earning brownie points in heaven, or being better than other people, or avoiding judgmental lightning bolts from the sky. Living free from sin is better for you and those around you, and that's why you should do it. Period.

If you need to have a funeral for yourself—for your old self—go right ahead. Take up your cross, as Jesus said, and follow him. Lose your life to gain your life. It might hurt during the process, but it will be worth it. When you die to who you used to be, you'll discover who you were created to be.

TWELVE

It's Okay to Change Your Mind: Losing Certainty

As a kid I loved bubble gum. I adored all the flavors, all the variations, all the presentations of gum. Well, except for grape. That one just didn't sit right with me. Assuming it was a nongrape flavor, though, I could chew and blow bubbles with a piece of gum for hours, until it turned into a hard, condensed little chunk of whatever gum is made out of. Then finally I'd throw it away.

One day as I was happily blowing bubbles, a woman came up to me and said, "Young man, be careful not to swallow that gum, because if you do, it'll take seven years to digest." I assumed that since she was an adult, she must know what she was talking about, so her words sent me into a panic. She scared the wintery fresh taste right out of my mouth. After that I stopped chewing gum altogether.

Her words stuck with me for years, like Velcro. Or like gum, actually. One day, though, I found myself wondering if that was even true. So I looked it up online. Guess what? Gum will typically pass right through you. It's gone from your body in hours, or maybe in a day or two. That's a lot less than seven years.

I'm still working on forgiving that woman. Okay, not really. It wasn't that big of a deal. But it is a little annoying to think about how many years I missed out on bubble gum because of a lie, a myth. Finding out that I had been misled was unsettling, and it forced me to rethink what I had assumed to be true. Needless to say, I had to stop being certain about something I had never questioned before.

Beliefs about bubble gum don't matter that much in the grand scheme of life, but there are a lot of other beliefs that do. Often these get turned into doctrinal debates or political talking points, but at the heart they are about how we see the world and other people. The crazy thing is, you can usually find smart, experienced, good people with contradictory opinions on just about any topic you choose. I'm not saying it's easy to figure out what is right or wrong. Truth is complex and nuanced. I'm just saying be willing to change your mind, and be intentional about learning and growing.

At first it might be difficult to give up what you always believed to be true. It's never easy to find out you've been wrong about something, especially if it's a lot more important than bubble gum and you were heart-and-soul invested in it. Questioning a truth you thought was absolute can feel sad, scary, and destabilizing. It can feel like death.

That's my point: you will often need to acknowledge, grieve, and let go of false assumptions and wrong ways of thinking. In other words, you need to hold a funeral for *certainty*. By that I don't mean you have to give up all certainty, of course. I'm referring to specific topics or beliefs that you used to have figured out, but now you're realizing you didn't know as much as you thought you did.

That can be incredibly unsettling, so your brain will likely jump into defensive mode right away. We tend to hold to our beliefs very stubbornly. A bit like toddlers. If you are a parent of a small child, you probably know what I mean. Changing the mind of a kid in this particular stage of life is an exercise in futility.

For example, have you ever tried to convince a toddler that they are tired and it is bedtime? That's an argument you won't win. Our son, Max, will use every excuse in the world to stay up, from having to use the bathroom to needing to take his vitamins. If there is a crack of hope, he will stick his hands in it and wedge it open. Small children can be falling asleep on their feet, yawning every five seconds, and having full-on emotional meltdowns because one sock fell off, but they'll still insist they are *not* tired and do *not* need to go to bed. They'll keep arguing right up until they fall asleep midsentence. And then you'll look at that peacefully sleeping face, kiss their sticky little forehead, and make a mental note to start the bedtime process earlier tomorrow.

When it comes to changing our minds, we often have the same stubbornness (and the same lack of emotional intelligence) as toddlers. We're right, and we know it, and heaven help the person who tries to tell us otherwise.

It's Hard to Be Wrong

The problem is that we are often not right. Or to use a phrase we prefer to avoid, *we are wrong*. We are human, and humans are finite and fallible. We need to get used to admitting we are wrong. Being wrong is one of the hallmarks of being human.

In any argument or disagreement, we are probably not completely wrong, of course. We are intelligent, and our experiences and points of view matter. But we also don't have all the facts, which means there's a high probability we are at least partly wrong. We tend to ignore that minor detail, though, and we argue

> **Being wrong is one of the hallmarks of being human.**

115

until we are blue in the face (and they don't have all the facts either). We wonder how everybody could be so ignorant when the truth is so obvious. Meanwhile they are wondering the same thing about us. Pretty soon the conversation devolves into a battle of wits (or lack thereof) that contains more snark and insults than actual facts.

Does that sound familiar? It feels like everywhere you turn people are arguing. Posting. Commenting. Fighting. Defending. Insulting. It can be exhausting, honestly.

At the same time, truth matters. God is true, after all, and he wants us to walk in truth. Jesus said he is the way, the truth, and the life (John 14:6). He said that we would know the truth, and the truth would set us free (John 8:32). Truth matters to God, so truth should matter to us.

If we're going to recognize our human fallibility but also value truth, we have to be willing to change our minds. It's that simple. We must admit that maybe, possibly, conceivably, perchance, we could be wrong. If we can't accept that we could be wrong about something, we'll never be open to learning what is right. We'll just defend our limited points of view like an annoyed, exhausted toddler.

Giving up a wrong belief can feel painful. It can feel like a loss, and it is: a loss of certainty. But it's a necessary loss. We must be willing to die to lies and half-truths, to wrong assumptions and erroneous conclusions, to harmful beliefs and toxic philosophies. We must learn to bury ideas we once cherished, then figure out how to do life differently.

Easier said than done. Everything within us—our emotions, our reflexes, our egos, our survival instinct—will try to defend what we think is right. It's a trait built into human nature. Most of us are quick to make up our minds and slow to change them. Why? Pride, maybe, or stubbornness, or fear. Likely, it's a combination of all the above. The point is, it's hard to let go of past beliefs or to recognize we could be wrong. It's not easy to open our minds to new things, to unlearn in order to relearn.

And yet—it's so freeing.

It's humbling to have to say, "I'm sorry. I was wrong," but it's so good for the soul. There is a lightness, a freedom, that comes when we clean out the lies and return to truth. Being wrong hurts us and those around us. So why would we want to hold on to a myth, a lie, a mistake?

Think back to your last argument with a loved one. No matter what the disagreement was initially about, there's a good chance that one or both of you dug in your heels and defended your position as if the fate of the world hung in the balance. You were right, after all, and they were wrong. It would be a travesty of justice to back down. A blasphemy against the truth. So you doubled down, raised your volume, and insisted they acknowledge your infallible and totally objective point of view.

Eventually—hopefully—love and humility won out. Your emotions calmed down, common sense kicked in, and you apologized for blowing things out of proportion. Maybe you realized that you were wrong about a thing or two. Perhaps you remembered that there are no infallible and totally objective points of view, because we are all simply doing the best we can to make sense of the world as we see it.

Once the storm clouds of stubbornness cleared, you both probably saw more clearly than before. You didn't simply compromise or meet in the middle either. You didn't just agree to disagree. Rather, you began to see the situation through the eyes of the other person. As a result, you grew. You changed. You expanded your perspective and understanding, not just of the situation itself but of the person you were arguing with and yourself as well.

You might not have come to full agreement. That's okay. But if you were able to humbly learn from the other person, if you were able to discard wrong perspectives and learn new ideas, if you made them think and they made you think, that's a win.

Be Willing to Think a Little Deeper

It's one thing to go into an "intense conversation" (a.k.a. argument) with a mind that is open enough to let somebody else in. That's good, and hopefully you're able to do this when you disagree with a friend or loved one.

It's another thing, though, to be willing to question your own deeply held beliefs or core values. That's a deeper level of open-mindedness, and it's one we should all aspire to. We have to be willing to question, challenge, tweak, discard, or expand the underlying worldviews we filter life through.

I'm not talking about redefining truth or saying everything is relative. Don't get me wrong. There is such a thing as truth, and all truth comes from God. The apostle John wrote, "God is light; in him there is no darkness at all. If we claim to have fellowship with him and yet walk in the darkness, we lie and do not live out the truth" (1 John 1:5–6). Everything about God is right, true, and perfect. It's light, not darkness. We are called to walk in that light, to walk according to his truth. The Bible itself is God's gift of truth to us, and we are responsible to understand and apply it. Not carelessly, though, or for selfish gain. Rather, with integrity, love, and a commitment to truth.

The problem is that we carry our human fallibility into every attempt to understand truth. Even our interpretations of the Bible are likely to contain some error. That doesn't undermine the Bible, or God, or truth itself. Instead, it reminds us that we need to stay humble. We need to accept that we might be wrong. We need to be willing to change our minds.

Some people seem incapable of doing this. No matter what facts they are presented with, no matter how many people tell them they are wrong, and no matter what consequences their wrong beliefs have caused, they refuse to rethink what they hold so dear. It feels threatening to them, like the ground they've always stood on is suddenly moving. If this belief falls, they subconsciously assume, then everything falls. Nothing will be solid or real or true. So they panic on the inside, raise their fists, and fight to the death for whatever they believe is true.

This is urgent, my friend. Wrong beliefs can harm people. The values and worldviews we cling to have wide-ranging effects on real humans. That should make us stop and think. It should make us seek wisdom, understanding, and knowledge, as the book of Proverbs so passionately exhorts us. If we dig in our heels to defend a pet doctrine; or we put our political views above the needs of people; or we propagate cultural, ethnic, gender, or racial stereotypes; or we fearmonger to justify and protect our lifestyles; or we weaponize Christianity to hold on to the world we've built for ourselves, we are building our lives on lies.

So often, the viewpoints we most loudly defend are human ones. We might quote a few Bible verses, but often our interpretations and applications of those verses are suspiciously approving of our lifestyles. We must learn to think critically. We must be humble enough to look at our own stances on topics with a distrusting eye, asking ourselves if we've allowed any error to creep in. Do we believe this way because it's right—or because it's easy? Are we defending the truth—or our privilege? Are we acting in love—or self-preservation?

I'm not attacking anyone here, and I'm not trying to be controversial. If you read the news, there are countless viewpoints on a myriad of topics, and most people are screaming at one another so loudly that nobody can hear themselves think. I'm not trying to wade into those battles.

Instead, I'm aiming deeper: At the mindsets that make us scream in the first place. At the pride and fear that motivate us to hold on to dead ideas, dead beliefs, dead prejudices, dead theories, and dead assumptions.

Love Is the Best Reason to Change

Few people are brave enough to question their core beliefs on their own. We are too deeply invested. When faced with the idea that we might be wrong about something, we usually try everything else first: denial, justification, blaming others, gaslighting, and more. We tend to give up wrong beliefs only when we have to, and that happens for one of two reasons: either reality forces us to from the outside or love changes us on the inside.

The first one, being forced to change our minds, reminds me of toddlers who are caught by sleep midsentence. They deny reality until reality knocks them over. Literally. Sometimes we hold on to a lie against all logic and evidence, until truth steamrolls us. Maybe we lose our jobs, or we lose friends, or we get sued, or we lose our credibility. We shouldn't have had to go through all that, but because we refused to learn and grow, we ended up facing the consequences.

Toddlers can get away with denying reality, but as adults, we need to be more self-aware. We need to be able to read the signs of the times, like Jesus told the religious leaders of the day. We must look at evidence and listen to a variety of voices until we get a bigger picture of what God is doing—not shrink our world until the only voices we allow are those who believe the same thing we do.

God cares about people. Deeply. So when our lies or misperceptions are hurting people, God has a way of bringing truth to the forefront. If we insist on holding on to ideas from the past when God is moving us forward, we are in for a rude awakening. It might not happen right away, but eventually we'll be left behind. We'll be excluded from what God is doing because we chose to protect a past we thought would last forever.

Many of the religious rulers of Jesus' day did exactly that. They defended their wrong interpretations of the Law to the one who wrote the Law. They trumpeted their skewed vision of the Messiah rather than the actual Messiah. Ultimately, they were left behind by the God they claimed to be following.

It's a sobering warning to us. We can't be so sure we have the truth that we forget to be learners.

Rather than being steamrolled by reality, a better way to change is through love. Love is a proactive strategy to keep growing in truth. When we choose to filter our thoughts through love, when we engage empathy *before* making up our minds, when we listen to people instead of just talking at them, everything changes. We see the world through bigger eyes, and it makes us slower to judge and quicker to embrace. Love forces us to confront our small-mindedness. It brings our selfish motives to the forefront, disables them, and then fills us with the compassion that always seemed to characterize Jesus.

Read what Paul had to say about love in 1 Corinthians 13:4–7. Don't apply this just to your relationships with your family or friends; apply it to whatever cultural topic or debate is most on your mind (or makes you the most nervous).

Love is patient, love is kind. It does not envy, it does not boast, it is not proud. It does not dishonor others, it is not self-seeking, it is not easily angered, it keeps no record of wrongs. Love does not delight in evil but rejoices with the truth. It always protects, always trusts, always hopes, always perseveres.

What if you chose to see people through this filter? What if, instead of debating others, you listened to them? What if, instead of labeling them, you loved them? What if, instead of demonizing them, you deferred to them? What if, instead of leading with certainty, you led with curiosity?

Don't make life about being right. Make it about love.

You don't have to agree with people in order to love them. They have a lot to learn from you too. But rather than insisting that everyone else change, why don't you change first? Be the quickest learner. Be the first to admit your mistakes. Be the most humble, the most open, the most loving. That would most accurately represent the love and grace of Jesus, don't you think?

Love will lead you to the truth because love will lead you to people: people made in the image of God, the very image of truth.

Don't make life about being right. Make it about love.

Part II: Processional

QUESTIONS FOR REFLECTION

Chapter 7. The Worst Hurt: Losing People

1. Have you experienced the death of a loved one? If so, how did that make you feel? How did you work through your loss?

2. Have you experienced little deaths when it comes to people, such as betrayal, breakups, moving away, or some other circumstance that ended a close relationship? How did the pain feel, and how long did it last? How did you process your loss and find healing?.

3. What advice would you give someone who is going through the loss of a person in some way, either physically or relationally?

Chapter 8. Sadly Ever After: Losing Dreams

1. Have you ever had a business venture or other important project fail? How did that make you feel? How did you respond?

2. How can you keep dreaming even after you've experienced loss or failure?

3. How does your awareness of God and your faith in him help you deal with broken dreams?

Chapter 9. When the Ground Shakes: Losing Security

1. Have you ever lost your job or another important source of income? How did that affect you? What did you learn from it?

2. What makes you feel insecure? What makes you feel secure? Do you need to make any adjustments in these things?

3. Can you think of a time where faith in God helped you navigate uncertain or unstable seasons?

Chapter 10. Spinning Out and Letting Go: Losing Control

1. Would you consider yourself someone who needs to be in control? Is that a good thing or a bad thing?

2. What areas of your life are under control? What areas seem to easily get out of control?

3. When life feels out of control, does your faith in God help you find peace? Practically speaking, how do you find peace in times of storm?

Chapter 11. New Sheriff in Town: Losing Sin

1. Are there any areas of character or sin that God might be asking you to work on? How did he reveal those areas to you? How is he helping you change?

2. How could love help you overcome character issues or temptations you might struggle with?

3. How can you become a more loving person?

Chapter 12. It's Okay to Change Your Mind: Losing Certainty

1. Can you think of a time you had to change your mind about something important? If so, how did that feel? Are you glad you did?

2. Is it difficult for you to admit when you are wrong? Why or why not? Does it matter whom you are admitting it to?

3. How do you react when a belief or idea is challenged? Do you believe that is the best way to react?

PART III
Eulogy
Commemoration

At a funeral the eulogy is about commemoration. The officiant, family, and friends speak about who the deceased was, how they lived, and what they left behind. This is a special moment because the person who has passed away becomes present again—not in their physical body but in their influence and the memories they created. It's a time to memorialize and honor what has been lost and to process grief in a healthy way.

> After the minister finishes his opening prayer, he invites the congregation to stand and sing a classic hymn of hope. It's an emotional moment as family and friends join their voices together in faith. The casket in front of them is never forgotten, but the reality of heaven begins to permeate the room. Death is not the end, the hymn affirms; it's only a beginning.
>
> After the hymn, the congregation is seated, and the pastor

reads a passage from the Bible, followed by a short message. Death is an enemy, he says, but it won't last forever. It has already been defeated by Jesus, and someday we will be reunited. Faith, hope, and love will prevail.

Then the minister begins to remember the person's life. This is the eulogy, the heart of the service. People lean forward in interest. Everyone knows the deceased in some way, but only in parts. Now they will get a fuller picture of the person they are here to commemorate.

The pastor goes through the key moments: date and place of birth, childhood years, education, career, marriage, children, church, and social involvement. Peppered through the description are anecdotes about the person who is being remembered: their sense of humor, their quirks, their hobbies, their family. Much is made of their accomplishments, of course: the way they helped people, their service to the community, their generosity. Some of their struggles are mentioned as well, briefly, because life isn't always easy, but perseverance is to be celebrated.

The effect in the room is almost tangible. People alternately laugh, cry, and ponder as they work through the memories that are left behind. Grief is a complex process, and saying goodbye is not straightforward. It is emotional, cyclical, organic. But there is peace in finding closure, and there is hope in contemplating the future.

In God, both life and death can be fully embraced.

Facing our loss is ultimately healing, but it's also complicated. In these next chapters, we explore ways to have a healthy perspective on loss and grief, including the *nuance* and complexity of loss; the reality and validity of the *pain* involved; the overwhelming nature of *emotions*; the importance of *timing* and moving on; the *resilience* built into our souls; and the healing power of *forgiveness*.

Part III - Eulogy: Commemoration

A funeral eulogy is a time to reflect on the deceased, and that's what we're going to do: sit with our loss, in all of its messiness and emotion, and give ourselves space to process our new reality. We'll look at how much it costs and how much it hurts to say goodbye, but we'll also discover the grace of God in the middle of loss. We'll find hope in heartbreak and faith in times of storm. Most of all, we'll discover how love will see us through.

THIRTEEN

Shades of Blue

No one has ever heard me speak publicly about what I'm about to share with you. It's difficult to talk about for a couple of reasons. First, because it reminds me of something I'd rather forget, and talking about it brings a wave of pain back to the surface. And second, because I wonder what anyone who reads this book will think of me. Silly, I know, but shame is a powerful thing.

I've been divorced before.

Just writing those words is intimidating and vulnerable, especially as a pastor. If you have been divorced or have gone through a relationship disappointment, you know what I'm talking about. There are layers of complexity and difficulty that are hard to understand yourself, much less explain to others.

I always knew that divorce is common, but I never thought it would happen to *me*. Without going into detail, I'll simply say that things didn't work out in my first marriage the way I had intended. When the relationship ended, I didn't know how to handle it. It wasn't just disappointing. It was heartbreaking. It was devastating. I have come to understand that divorce is one of the few times in life when we mourn the loss of someone who is still alive. It felt so contradictory and confusing at the time.

Although that season was heartbreaking and difficult for me to process and understand, God wrapped his hands around my heart and protected me from the severity of what I could have felt. I'm not saying I didn't suffer—it was incredibly difficult. But in the suffering, God was present, and that was enough.

Yet out of that great pain came the greatest blessing. I was able to meet my wife, Jennifer. God has blessed me beyond what I could have imagined back then, and his grace and goodness are on full display in my life.

I am sharing my story to remind you that, in any loss, there are both good and bad pieces all mixed together, and it can be hard to separate them. Sometimes things don't turn out how we expected. But as Romans 8:28 reminds us, God takes the good and the bad and makes them work together for those who love him. If you've gone through a divorce, or if you're going through something else that feels just as devastating and confusing, please know that there is life on the other side.

I said earlier that shame is a powerful thing. I wish that weren't true, but it is. Here's the deal, though. While you shouldn't live with constant shame, you can't expect it to magically go away, totally and forever, just because you want it to. Instead, you have to continually resist it, dismantle it, and overcome it. How? By remaining open and vulnerable. In her book *Dare to Lead*, researcher and author Brené Brown wrote, "When we find the courage to share our experiences and the compassion to hear others tell their stories, we force shame out of hiding and end the silence. . . . Shame derives its power from being unspeakable."[1] Don't let shame stop you from moving forward, or from trying again, or from opening up to others. Instead, learn to overcome it by moving toward vulnerability and love.

If shame gets its power from silence, then healing gets its power from openness. That's what we're doing by holding funerals, after all. We're admitting that some things didn't work as planned. For whatever reason—or, more likely, for many reasons—we went through a loss or disappointment that wasn't on our radar. Now we're picking up the pieces, and the last thing we need is the voice of shame beating us down. Instead, we need to open our hearts, our minds, and our mouths and start working through the many layers of loss.

Whether it's the death of a marriage, a dream, an opportunity, or anything else that is near and dear to us, this kind of loss is often complicated and confusing. Not only that, but every loss is unique. You can't put every pain on the same timeline or describe them all using the same words. Each death—just like each life—is different. To talk about death and disappointment, then, we must discuss complexity.

Nuance Is Sacred

One of my favorite words to describe complexity is *nuance*. Nuance refers to the subtle distinctions or shades of meaning in something. It means that a topic, a truth, a situation, or even a person can have layers. There might be more to them than meets the eye. They can be complex, chaotic, hard to summarize.

Take colors as an example. If you tell a fashion designer or interior designer you're looking for something blue, they'll probably stare at you, roll their eyes, or laugh outright and then hit you with some follow-up questions. "Exactly what shade of blue did you have in mind?" "How light, how dark, how bright?" "What mood are you trying to set?" "What feeling are you going for?" "Where will this be used?" That simple word *blue* covers an incredibly wide range of hues and shades: baby blue, navy blue, neon blue, electric blue, midnight blue, powder blue, periwinkle blue, ultramarine blue, sapphire blue, and hundreds more. That is nuance.

Or think about coffee, wine, and cheese. Those broad categories are only a starting point. If you talk to a barista, sommelier, or turophile (that's a cheese fanatic—I looked it up), someone who has the palette and vocabulary to describe what you're tasting, you'll discover a world of flavors you didn't know existed. That is nuance.

Difficult things can have nuance too. Your pain has nuance. Your loss has nuance. Your disappointment has nuance. Your grief has nuance. Your death experiences have layers, and those layers matter.

Nuance is one reason deaths can be so arduous to process. Wave after wave of different emotions—sometimes contradictory ones—wash over us. That's okay. It's normal. Rather than trying to oversimplify your loss, let yourself feel the emotions. Examine the layers one at a time. Recognize the beauty and the pain that are woven together.

For example, maybe the death you're going through is the loss of a romantic relationship, and the person was perfect for you in many ways—but in others, not so much. Now you're left with some glorious memories and a few toxic ones. You miss the person, but you're hurt by them too. You're glad they're gone and you wish they'd come back, all at once.

It would be easier if you could just be completely mad at them, or at least that's what your subconscious tells you. As a result, you find yourself rewriting history a little: highlighting the bad memories, erasing the good ones, trying to turn the person into a full-on villain so it's easier to stay mad at them.

But were they a villain? Or were they just human? And were you an angel, or were you simply human too?

One time the apostle Paul was dealing with criticism from others, and instead of defending himself, he made a couple of interesting statements. First, he said, "I care very little if I am judged by you or by any human court; indeed, I do not even judge myself. My conscience is clear, but that does not make me innocent. It is the

Lord who judges me" (1 Corinthians 4:3–4). He wasn't going to lose sleep over the criticism, because he was as sure as humanly possible that he wasn't the terrible person he was being painted as. He wasn't standing on his own conscience, though. Rather, he was open to God's correction and direction. That's an interesting mix of humility and confidence.

Then he added this: "Therefore judge nothing before the appointed time; wait until the Lord comes. He will bring to light what is hidden in darkness and will expose the motives of the heart. At that time each will receive their praise from God" (v. 5). What was he saying? Basically that it's impossible to completely know what people's motives are, including our own. We should do our best to act with integrity, of course, but ultimately God is the only one who can see into our hearts and discern right from wrong. Interestingly, when he does that, "each will receive their praise from God." Paul didn't even mention criticism or judgment here, just praise. That's because God isn't out to rebuke everyone for every little mistake; instead, he's mainly going to highlight and celebrate what we got right.

When it comes to how we treat others, we need this same humble recognition that we are not God. We can't see their hearts. We don't always know what actions were good or bad, what words were true or false, what motives were pure or flawed. Yes, we should do our best to be wise and observant, but we also need to scale back our tendency to pass quick and final judgment on everyone. We need to recognize that most things are more complicated than they seem at first glance and that layers and nuances matter.

The temptation to erase nuance is a dangerous one. If you revise the past, you can't mourn it properly. Plus, you end up demonizing people (or yourself) instead of acknowledging that good and bad coexisted, as they always do. Besides all that, you won't be able to learn from the entire experience, both the good and the bad.

I've started a few different businesses and entrepreneurial endeavors over the years, and I've always considered myself to be relatively savvy in business. There was one particular project I was excited and passionate about, an investment in a certain technology that I thought would do really well. It didn't, though, and I ended up losing my entire investment. That made me feel like a failure, but even worse, it meant I couldn't make some other investments I had planned.

It took me a while to work through the emotions and the consequences of that, but I came out stronger on the other side. The pain itself was a motivation to analyze what went wrong, to learn, and to be more cautious in the future. As a result, I approached future investment opportunities with more wisdom. It was a loss, but it was a loss that became a win—which is what should always happen if we're willing to see the big picture.

If you're going through a death experience, or if you are still mourning something that died in the past, take a few minutes to celebrate the nuance. Peel back the layers and see if you have a full, healthy perspective.

Have you idealized something or someone you lost to the point that you are overlooking things that were genuinely harmful? To some degree, it's normal for the good memories to outlast the bad: time has a way of healing wounds and covering sins. But if you are still limping from hurts you haven't allowed yourself to admit exist, you need to be honest about it. Take time to find healing. You can still love and respect someone who caused you harm. You can still be grateful for jobs, dreams, and opportunities that blessed your life in some way, even if there are elements of those seasons you wish you could redo.

On the other hand, have you demonized something because you lost it? Have you allowed the negative memories to define that thing or that person, even though there were some positive ones as well? If so, allow yourself to feel grateful for the good times you had. Don't feel guilty for that. You gave a part of yourself to that season. You were invested. You took risks. You made yourself vulnerable. Whatever good came out of it should be celebrated, even if the end of the season was not what you would have chosen.

You don't have to classify and label everything that happened into *good* or *bad*. Sometimes it can simply exist. It can just be a thing that happened because life is messed up like that. Now you're better for it—but maybe a little worse too. So you thank God for the good and get therapy for the bad. I'm kidding. Well, mostly.

"Nuance is sacred work," wrote rapper Propaganda,[2] and he's right. When we are humble and brave enough to see both the good and the bad in life, we reflect God's heart more closely. God doesn't oversimplify us. And he doesn't oversimplify what we are going through. He sees it all and holds it all: the good, the bad, the ugly, the embarrassing, the hilarious, the odd, the awesome.

Try to look at life (and death) the same way. Don't oversimplify it. Don't erase the details or ignore the layers. Instead, embrace all of it, even the parts you don't understand, and look for God in the nuance.

Nothing Is a Waste

This concept of nuance means something else: not everything that looks like failure is ultimately failure. Put another way, sometimes you don't see the blessings of something until it's gone. Paul likely had something like that in mind when he told the Corinthians not to judge anything before its time.

Don't be too quick to write things off as tragic, horrible mistakes. Just because something died doesn't mean it never should have lived. And just because it didn't end how you expected doesn't mean you did something wrong. You have to be able to hold both the good and the bad at the same time or you'll tend to let the pain of your loss overwhelm the gifts you've received—or the future that remains to be written.

Romans 8:28 is one of the greatest truths in the Bible: "And we know that in all things God works for the good of those who love him, who have been called according to his purpose." Read that again.

In *all* things.

God works.

For our good.

When God is in charge, there is usually more happening than meets the eye. You might have gone through an ending, but that's not necessarily the end. What others might call failure can still work for your good. What feels like loss can ultimately be your gain. Years in the future, you'll probably look back on what you're walking through today and be grateful for some of it. Maybe most of it. You'll realize then what you can't see now: that things are working for your good. Even the bad ones. Even the sad ones. Even the hurtful ones. Out of the ashes of the past, something new comes into being.

> **Out of the ashes of the past, something new comes into being.**

How can that be? How can good come from evil? There are countless possibilities, of course. Here are a few of the "new" things that tend to rise from the ashes of the old:

1. New doors

    It's painful to watch a door close, especially if you are deeply invested in what you are losing. Maybe it's a boyfriend you hoped to marry or a business idea you thought would make millions. When that door closes, though, it frees up time and energy to pursue other opportunities. What doors are opening around you? What opportunities have you never noticed that now seem worth exploring? Maybe what you lost was actually more of a distraction than a blessing.

2. New friends

We noted earlier that relational loss is the hardest pain to deal with because people are not replaceable. However, that doesn't mean you won't find new friendships. You can miss the people you lost and still love the people you meet. The human heart has a massive capacity to love, after all. Are there people around you whom you could reach out to? How could you be friendlier or more intentional about building a friend group?

3. New growth

I know it's not fun to hear this when you're going through pain, but suffering does build character, and character matters more than we usually admit. As the saying goes, "What doesn't kill you makes you stronger," right? Someday you'll look back on this season and be amazed at how you grew in faith, compassion, wisdom, and courage. Inner growth is more important than external growth, so don't overlook what's happening inside you.

4. New ideas

To quote another old saying, "Necessity is the mother of invention." There's nothing like a little desperation to spark creativity. Maybe this loss is what you needed to think outside the box or to pursue a direction you hadn't considered. Maybe you'll realize you need to study more, get better advice, or build a team. Then you'll go into your next business, relationship, ministry, or goal with the added benefit of having learned from the past. You didn't fail—you tried. And now you're going to try again.

Time Machines Are Overrated

When I think back to certain mistakes I've made in business or leadership, I have mixed feelings. Part of me wishes I could go back in time and change a few things. That would mean I could skip the pain, save the money, and avoid the embarrassment that comes with failure. However, another part of me is genuinely grateful for the good that came out of those mistakes. To be honest, I don't know what I'd do if I were offered a time machine. The valuable lessons I've learned, my growth as a person, the wisdom I've acquired—I am grateful for those things, and I'd miss them if they were gone.

I know that's confusing. But that's the whole point of nuance. When something bad happens, it's tempting to write the entire area off as a total loss. *Wow, that job didn't work out. That boyfriend was a loser. That business idea was stupid. That dream was a joke. That project was a waste of time.* Then you throw it in the trash and try to forget it happened.

But it's too early to write it all off as failure. It's usually better to put things on the shelf for a while. Don't make up your mind too quickly. Don't pass judgment too severely. Give space and grace for God to work things together for good. This is nuance in action. You have to be able to look under the surface a little, to see past the pain and notice the progress being made.

God tends to work quietly. Sneakily. Unexpectedly. When the time is right, he's going to do something you couldn't have dreamed up yourself, something that wouldn't have happened if things had worked out "right" the first time.

He'll probably use some of the pieces of your broken dream. He might pull in some of the people you've met along the way. He'll definitely use some of the skills you picked up and the character you built. That's how God works. In him, nothing is a waste.

Not even death.

FOURTEEN

Ice Baths for the Soul

Wim Hof, also known as the Iceman, is a Dutch extreme athlete known for his ability to withstand cold temperatures. He set the Guinness World Record for running the fastest half-marathon barefoot on ice or snow (2 hours, 16 minutes, 34 seconds).[1] He also set the world record for the longest ice bath (1 hour, 52 minutes, 42 seconds). He climbed 19,340-foot Mount Kilimanjaro wearing only shorts and shoes. In total, he has claimed twenty-six world records for his extreme stunts.[2]

I like sports and competition, but that is next-level. It's borderline insane, if you ask me. The most unbelievable thing, though, is that Wim Hof insists all of us are capable of this sort of endurance. He wrote in his book *The Wim Hof Method*, "I am no superhero. I am no genetic freak. . . . Anything I can do, you can do just as well."[3]

But do we want to, Mr. Hof? That's the question.

The Wim Hof Method is not just about climbing snowy mountain peaks in less clothing than most of us wear to bed at night. Instead, it claims to help with chronic-pain management, inflammation, stress, autoimmune disorders, and a host of other ailments. It focuses on dealing with pain not by ignoring it or medicating it but by gaining greater control of your body and mind, by digging into reservoirs of human resilience you didn't know you had. How? Mostly by taking ice baths and breathing a lot. So far I haven't gotten up the nerve to try it.

Why do I mention all this? Because Wim Hof knows what countless other athletes—both extreme athletes and "normal" ones—understand: that we are capable of far more than we think we are. That often our limitation is not our physical body but our pain tolerance. That if we can get in the right frame of mind, we can accomplish things that seem superhuman to others.

Pain is a normal part of death experiences. When we suffer loss or experience disappointment, we naturally feel pain. That pain can feel overwhelming at times. We might think there is no way we can make it through. That somehow we have to stop the pain, hide from the pain, or medicate the pain.

Sometimes, though, we just have to walk through the pain. We must learn to sit with discomfort. We need to dig into the reservoirs of our souls and find strength and control we didn't know we had.

I don't mean that in a dismissive way. If you're suffering through a death experience right now, your pain is real. My point is not that pain is "all in your head" or that you should "just tough it out," but rather that you are capable of conquering more than you realize, and you are stronger than you think.

You're Stronger Than You Think

Pain will make you feel weak. It will tell you that you are a wimp, a loser, a failure. But don't fall for that. You are not weak—pain is. All pain can do is make you hurt. It can't control your destiny, your attitude, your faith, or your future. Therefore you are stronger than pain.

Yes, pain hurts. That's the literal definition of pain. But, generally speaking, it doesn't kill you. It might make you think you're going to die, but that's just a scare tactic so that you'll take care of whatever is wrong.

Pain is meant to help you by pointing out what needs to change. If you sprain your ankle, the pain is there so you won't put weight on it and make it worse. Pain is your friend, but it's like that one friend we all have who has only one volume: loud. Everything is drama. Everything is urgent. Everything is worth yelling about.

The problem is that when you are in pain because you lost something you cared deeply about, there's not a lot you can do to take the pain away. Though pain is yelling in your ear, you can't shut it up by fixing the problem. A death has occurred, and death is not fixable.

In that case, the pain is probably not telling you to fix something. It might, however, be telling you to take care of your *soul*. To not rush past the hurt, because if you do, you could end up damaging yourself in invisible ways.

Let the pain remind you to grieve. Walk—or limp—through the complex process of saying goodbye to the past and reimagining the future. You can expect a significant amount of pain during that process. It will diminish with time, of course. But grief has its own timetable and its own healing process.

Too often we try to deal with pain the wrong way. Maybe we run from it, ignore it, or push through it. Perhaps we deny it or medicate ourselves with alcohol or drugs. We might grow bitter or let our world get smaller and smaller as we shut people out.

But pain doesn't have to do any of that to us. We are bigger than pain. We are stronger than loss. There are deep reservoirs of resilience within us, but we have to tap into them.

The Bible speaks many times of courage, faith, hope, and strength. Often those words are given in the context of suffering and sorrow. These are themes throughout the Bible because they are themes throughout humanity. That means you are not alone. Your suffering is real, but you can access the same grace and strength that countless people before you have found in God.

The apostle Peter wrote, "Resist [the devil], standing firm in the faith, because you know that the family of believers throughout the world is undergoing the same kind of sufferings. And the God of all grace, who called you to his eternal glory in Christ, after you have suffered a little while, will himself restore you and make you strong, firm and steadfast" (1 Peter 5:9–10).

Peter was reminding his readers that we all face suffering. That doesn't diminish anyone's pain; rather, it unites us more closely because of it. Even though we bear our own pain, we don't have to suffer alone. We have one another, and we have God, the "God of all grace." He's the God who called us and carries us, the God who will restore us, the God who makes us strong, firm, steadfast.

Find strength in God, in people around you, and deep in your soul.

My friend, *you can do this*. I know you can. The God of all grace is with you. Let courage rise within you. Make faith the only voice you listen to. Find strength in God, in people around you, and deep in your soul. In him, you are stronger than you think.

Put Pain in Perspective

In order to process pain in a healthy way, we need to have the right perspective on it. That's not easy, though, because pain itself skews our perspective.

Pain is real, but it's also a liar sometimes. Or at least a really effective exaggerator. By way of illustration, consider how kids respond when they get hurt. One of the constant questions parents find themselves asking is, "How bad are they hurt, really?" The parenting books don't talk about this, but it's real. If you're a parent, I know you feel me on this one.

For example, you hear a loud *thud* in the other room, followed by absolute silence. The silence might mean nothing is wrong, which is what you hope and pray for. It might mean something valuable broke, and your child is evaluating whether to run or confess. Or it might mean they are simply filling their lungs with air, because they are about to scream loud enough to make your neighbors call the police.

If the latter happens, you run to comfort them and assess the scene. It's parental triage at its finest. Is the child breathing? (Obviously they are because they are yelling at the top of their lungs.) Are they losing blood? Are all their body parts attached? Are they able to stand? Is that a real limp or a fake one? Is that a hurt cry or a mad cry or a tired cry?

Once you establish they are not in immediate danger, you have to figure out whether this injury will go away on its own or it needs medical intervention. So you interrogate them—lovingly.

"How bad does it hurt?"

"Terrible! Horrible! Worst pain ever."

"Where does it hurt?"

"Everywhere. My whole body hurts."

"What does it feel like?"

"Like a thousand knives are being stabbed into me."

"Can you move it?"

"No!" (screams)

"Does this hurt?"

"Don't touch me!"

"Can you walk?"

"I'll never walk again."

At this point, you realize questions are futile. All they are aware of is their pain, and pain is controlling all their answers.

So you put a bandage or ice on it, whichever seems most appropriate. You distract them with their favorite show and bribe them with ice cream. You give them time to calm down. Then, once the pain and panic and fear have subsided a bit, you decide whether they need to go to the ER and get X-rays, or if they just need a nap.

My point here is not to scare you off from having children. It's to remind you that kids are not the only ones who have trouble being objective about pain. *We all do.* When we are hurting, we interpret everything through the lens of pain.

The presence of pain has a way of drowning out logic and skewing perspective. It triggers automatic responses by our minds and bodies. We want to run. To hide. To fight. To do something, *anything*, that alleviates the pain.

Since pain is meant to get our attention, it has a way of demanding that we focus on it. It yells at us. It gnaws at us. It shouts in superlatives: *This is the worst! This is terrible! There is no hope! You're going to die! Everything is awful!*

If pain is yelling in your ear, do some personal triage. That is, look past the feelings and see what needs to be addressed. Ask yourself, *How real is this pain? How urgent is the problem? How dramatically and drastically should I respond? Do I need a nap? Would ice cream help?* Those are important questions. If you don't get a good perspective on your pain, you'll tend to react wrongly to it.

The last thing you want to do when you're hurting is compound your pain by making wrong decisions. This is all too common. I've done it, and you probably have too. Something happens that makes you sad, angry, scared, or confused, so you go out and do something stupid, probably to distract yourself from the pain. Maybe you write something angry on someone's social media, or you binge-eat eight thousand calories a day for a month, or you quit your job, or you blow up your marriage, or you buy something you definitely can't afford, or you wear socks with sandals in public. Doing things that cause pain in order to distract yourself from pain is not a good tactic, though. It's like hitting your finger with a hammer to distract yourself from a broken leg.

Our culture is quick to hate on pain. We do all we can to achieve a pain-free existence. But the reality is that pain is an inevitable part of our existence, at least this side of heaven. Instead of hating on it, we need to understand why it's there and what it's telling us.

Are you going through a death experience? Listen to your hurt. Sit with your sorrow. Make peace with your pain. Don't let it skew your perspective or control your responses. Don't ignore pain, and don't overreact to pain. Somewhere between those two extremes is where you need to be. If you need to, reach out to friends, or go to therapy, or spend some time praying, or take ice baths and breathe a lot if that's your thing.

You will get through this pain. It won't last forever, at least not at this level of intensity. Remember, there is more to you than you realize, more strength inside that you have yet to tap into. Keep going. You'll find a reservoir of faith and a well of hope. Most of all, you'll meet a God of grace.

FIFTEEN

Surfing Monsters

Have you ever watched big-wave surfing competitions? There are a number of these throughout the world, but maybe the most impressive one takes place in Portugal at a place called Nazaré. Google it. It's worth it.

The waves there are monsters that can reach eighty feet in height. Imagine surfing with an eight-story building crumbling and crashing right behind you. That's the stuff of nightmares for most of us, but these men and women do it *for fun*. I have mad respect for them while simultaneously worrying about their sanity. (Coincidentally and off topic, that's how I feel about parents of teenagers.)

Some of the time, these big-wave surfers wipe out. When they do, it's beyond epic. It looks like the entirety of Niagara Falls is crashing over them. That's dangerous, of course, so there are always multiple spotters on Jet Skis nearby. If someone gets destroyed by a wave, the driver's job is to locate the floundering surfer in the foam and waves, drive to wherever they are, then tow them out of the break zone—all before the next massive wave barrels through a few seconds later. It's intense, to put it mildly. Either "awesome-intense" or "terrifying-intense," depending on whether the surfer wins the battle or the wave does.

The exhilarating-but-terrifying rush that big-wave surfers experience reminds me of the emotional "waves" that usually accompany our death experiences. When going through difficult moments of loss and pain, we might feel like eighty-foot waves of fear, anxiety, sorrow, and anger are about to crash down on our heads, and we have to either hang on or die trying. If we stay on our metaphorical boards and ride it out, it's an experience we'll never forget. That takes courage, strength, balance, and skill. We might be scared to death, but we come out alive and proud of our grit. If the wave catches us off guard, though, the experience is totally different. We might find ourselves drowning in despair, grief, and doubt, struggling just to breathe while we figure out which way is up.

Keep in mind that while the Nazaré surfers have the *choice* of swimming out into the ocean or not, we do not have the same luxury when it comes to our emotional monster waves. Overwhelming waves of emotion are part of life, and we all find ourselves caught up in them from time to time. So if we're going to survive the emotional breakers that come our way, we'd better become skilled at handling them. And that starts with understanding them.

Death Isn't Supposed to Make Sense

Now, understanding emotions doesn't necessarily mean understanding why bad things happen. Emotions are confusing in themselves, but they are especially difficult to process when the event that caused them is confusing too. For example, if your best friend betrays you—maybe they lie about you, or divulge a secret, or steal your job, or start dating your ex—not only do you have to deal with grief and loss, but you also find yourself wondering why they, of all people, did that to you. Both the *loss* and the *emotions that follow the loss* are hard to navigate, and you can end up feeling overwhelmed.

I've officiated a number of funerals that were incredibly difficult because of the circumstances behind them. Most of them were for young people or adults who died unexpectedly, such as in a car wreck. In those instances, the grief and loss and pain were almost overwhelming, and they were compounded by the senselessness of the death. *Why did this happen to this person? It's not fair. It's not right. It doesn't make sense.*

Death never makes sense. Humans were not meant to die, after all. Death is an intrusion, an enemy. So a funeral must wrestle with the strange, painful paradox of accepting something we weren't built to accept. That's difficult to do. Impossible, maybe. Death might make sense once we get to heaven, but for now, it causes a lot of pain and confusion.

The same goes for our little death experiences, although on a smaller scale. It's hard to make sense of pain. It's difficult to reconcile suffering with faith. If God is good, present, and powerful, why is life so stinking hard? Why do we hurt so often and so much?

I don't pretend to know the answer to that. A lot of things are beyond my ability to understand, and bad things happening to good people is one of them. (Other conundrums for me include quantum physics, toddlers, and people who don't use turn signals.) I suspect heaven will help us see this life a lot more clearly, but in the meantime, we'd better get used to dealing with confusing emotions.

Speaking of heaven, the book of Revelation describes heaven as the undoing of those things that bring us the most confusion here on earth. John wrote, "'He will wipe every tear from their eyes. There will be no more death' or mourning or crying or pain, for the old order of things has passed away" (Revelation 21:4).

It's a beautiful promise about heaven, but it tells us a lot about earth too. Specifically that as long as we are on this planet, we're going to have to deal with death and pain. That means we'll have tears in our eyes at times, and we'll go through seasons of mourning. Things will not always make sense. We'll feel contradictory emotions and have contradictory thoughts.

If you feel angry or fearful or confused or hurt or betrayed because of a loss you've experienced, you're normal. You don't have to deny or stifle those feelings. But you also don't have to let them control you. The trick is to find the sweet spot between those two extremes.

Surfing Beats Sinking Every Time

How do we find this sweet spot? By learning to recognize and regulate our emotions. This is often called *emotional intelligence*, and it definitely comes in handy when life feels overwhelming. The good news is, emotional intelligence is a learned skill, so you can get better at it. The bad news is, you get better through practice. The more strong emotions you face, the better you get at handling them.

Easier said than done, you're probably thinking. And you're right. That's why my Nazaré experience is limited to the internet rather than actually getting on a board and trying it myself. I know my limits, and surfing enormous waves is far beyond that ceiling. For that matter, so is surfing any kind of waves. I'm more of a "stay close to shore and watch out for sharks" kind of guy than a "brave death by plummeting down the side of a watery cliff" one.

I'll leave surfing to the experts, but I can offer a few suggestions on how to deal with strong emotions without getting drowned by them.

Grieve without losing your love.

Anger is one of the most common emotions in the face of pain and loss. C. S. Lewis is often quoted as saying, "I sat with my anger long enough until she told me her real name was grief." In my experience, being upset is one of the first signs that I am mourning the loss of something. Either that or I'm hungry.

Paul wrote, "In your anger do not sin" (Ephesians 4:26). Stated another way, when you're mad, don't punch anyone in the face. Paul was talking about interpersonal conflicts here, but the same principle is true in any situation and for all emotions. You can and will feel things deeply. But that doesn't mean you should lash out and hurt other people.

How do you do that when eighty-foot waves of grief are pummeling you? By never losing sight of love. Grief and loss make us look at ourselves. That's okay, at least for a while. But they don't have to blind us to others. You can grieve and love at the same time. You can feel deep emotion while still considering the needs and feelings of other people. And you can be angry without causing harm.

You can grieve and love at the same time.

Hold off on assigning blame.

It's human nature to want to blame someone for our pain. Often, however, no one is at fault. Other times, everyone is a little bit at fault. And still others, it's impossible to know who is at fault. In short, assigning blame is not easy. If you're still grieving a loss, don't be in a hurry to decide who messed up and what they did wrong. Don't pass judgment too soon.

When your emotions subside, you'll be better equipped to decide. At that point, though, you might realize it doesn't matter. Nobody was out to get you. Nobody massively failed you. Nobody is your enemy. Life just hurts sometimes, and you needed time to mourn.

Other times, when the emotions die down a little, you realize you really were attacked, failed, or defrauded in some way. If that's the case, you likely need to take steps to address the situation. You'll still feel strong emotion, of course, but you'll make decisions from a place of self-control and wisdom.

Avoid getting stuck in bitterness.

Bitterness is different from sadness or anger. Those emotions come and go, but bitterness is a state of being. It's a decision to mentally and emotionally handcuff yourself to something painful. The problem with that, of course, is that if you're permanently attached to pain, you'll never heal.

I'm not saying to "just get over" the hurt you are feeling. Sometimes people flippantly say things like that because they are bothered by your pain or because they haven't empathized with your situation. That's not helpful.

Don't get over it—but don't get plowed under by it either. Even in pain and sorrow, even in loss and hurt, even in disappointment, you still have control over yourself. You have God-given autonomy. Choose to grieve for as long as you need, then choose to heal. Both are important, and both are within your power.

Keep your heart open and your world big.

Pain and loss can put you on the defensive; if you were blindsided by this tragedy, what's going to happen next? If you lost this dream, is anything safe? You had better hold on tighter to what you have, suspect everyone, and be ready to fight at a moment's notice. Or so you think.

A head-down-fists-up mentality will tend to shrink your world ever smaller, which is the last thing you want. That mindset won't help you, nor can it protect you. Ironically, it is not by holding on tighter that we find happiness but by becoming bigger and more generous. We save our lives by losing them, Jesus said (Luke 9:24).

You were created to love and believe. Death experiences will try to poison your heart and steal your faith, but that doesn't have to happen.

Refuse to become cynical or make everyone an enemy. Instead, let your grief and hurt deepen, widen, and broaden who you are.

Turn to Jesus.

This can sound cliché, but Jesus really does know your pain. We saw earlier how he wept with Mary and Martha when Lazarus died. I believe he weeps with us in our pain as well. Isaiah said this about Jesus: "He was despised and rejected by mankind, a man of suffering, and familiar with pain. . . . Surely he took up our pain and bore our suffering" (Isaiah 53:3–4).

Faith is most real and most needed in times of suffering. It's strange how often we try to shut down our emotions as if feeling anger or pain were somehow less spiritual. If you ever start to think that way, open your Bible to the book of Psalms. If anyone knew how to be real with what he was feeling, it was David. If you're still not convinced, read the book of Job. It's a dramatic, gory, in-your-face story of loss, tragedy, grief, complaints, anger, toxic friends, bad advice, hard questions, and ultimately God's graciousness. Another Old Testament book is literally named Lamentations. I could go on. Every book of the Bible speaks directly to the human experience in all its chaos and messiness. Every hero and heroine of the Bible had to overcome loss and pain.

Jesus is "familiar with pain." He doesn't judge you or reject you. He doesn't mock you, condemn you, or rebuke you. Instead, he embraces you. He binds up your wounds, strengthens your heart, and renews your hope.

From Nazaré to Nazareth

The big-wave surfers of Nazaré might be experts at their craft, but they can't compare to Jesus of Nazareth. He doesn't just surf the waves—he *stills* the waves. He speaks to storms and calms them with his voice. He isn't afraid of crashing waves, because he created the water they are made from, and he walks on their surface as if it were dry land.

In the same way, Jesus isn't afraid of your waves of fear, hurt, or anger. He created those emotions too. The same voice that stills the waves will bring peace to your heart. You might find yourself tossed about by some monster waves of emotion. You might feel confused at times, or afraid, or hurt. But the waves can't sink you. And they definitely can't drown you.

The waves will pass and calm will come. And through it all, Jesus is by your side.

SIXTEEN

Let Go of the Mic

Often at funerals, the family of the deceased will ask a few close friends or family members to make some remarks. And by "remarks," they mean taking two or three minutes to give a few loving comments about the deceased and perhaps share a brief anecdote if time allows.

At one funeral I was officiating, the family had three people on the schedule to give some words. The first person went forward and took the mic. He did great, and he stayed within his time. Then the second person went forward and did the same.

Finally the third person took the mic. He was an uncle of the deceased, and it quickly became clear that he had the spiritual gift of gab. Being mindful that he was a family member, I didn't say anything for a while, and he continued enthusiastically. After ten minutes, I finally stood up, walked over to him, and discreetly stood behind him. It was a polite hint that it was time to move on. He didn't take the hint.

After another five or ten minutes, things were getting awkward. Not only had he hijacked the service, but his comments had also veered way off topic. Finally I did what I always do when someone needs to relinquish the mic: I stood right next to him and tapped his shoulder. I call it a courtesy tap. It was a firm, unmistakable reminder that the time was up and he needed to give me back the mic.

He kept going.

By now it was getting bad. It was obvious to everyone that his comments were less about honoring the deceased or comforting the family and more about staying in the spotlight. People were visibly uncomfortable as the minutes ticked by. Eventually I had to physically remove the mic from his hand. Then I thanked him (insincerely) and invited him (firmly) to be seated.

The funeral proceeded without incident after that. Unfortunately, his refusal to respect the timing of the service soured the entire event. What should have been an opportunity to offer a short, touching tribute turned into a spectacle. Why? Because he dragged it on for way too long.

God Wants the Mic Back

That long-winded uncle isn't the only one guilty of hijacking funerals. I've realized that, often, we do the same thing when it comes to our death experiences. We mourn them, remember them, lament them—but we don't pay attention to the timing. We get stuck in grieving mode and refuse to move on.

Sooner or later, though, God wants the mic back. The funeral needs to keep moving. So he gently nudges us to let us know we're holding up the grieving process. He encourages us to let go and move forward. The burial needs to happen, but it can't if we insist on reliving the loss forever.

David famously wrote, "Even though I walk through the darkest valley, I will fear no evil, for you are with me" (Psalm 23:4). Other translations call it the "valley of the shadow of death" (e.g., NKJV).

Notice David talked about *walking through* the valley. He did not say, "Even though I build a house in the darkest valley and live here for the next twenty-five years."

Valleys of death and darkness are not meant to be long-term homes. They are meant to be traveled through, not inhabited permanently. That journey might take a while, but there should be progress. If we don't recognize and respect proper timing, we end up souring the experience. We make loss all about ourselves rather than understanding that life is bigger than just us.

But wait, you might be thinking. *Isn't loss about ourselves? Isn't that the point of grief? I lost something dear to me, so of course I'm going to feel sorrow.*

Yes, your sorrow is yours. Your pain is personal. But you don't grieve in a vacuum, alone and disconnected from the world. You exist within a larger context, and so do your pain and grief. The guy who wouldn't give up the mic refused to acknowledge his context. He was grieving in his own way, maybe—but it definitely wasn't helpful to anyone else.

The valley of darkness won't last forever.

In your pain, don't lose sight of your context. I'm not trying to tell you how to grieve, but I am telling you to remember you are still in the land of the living even when you're mourning the dead. The funeral is moving on. The burial must take place. The valley of darkness won't last forever. A wide, beautiful world awaits, and you are an integral part of it. Don't stand there clutching the mic for too long or you'll miss out on all that God has for you.

You actually pay more respect to the things you've lost by allowing them to be buried at the proper time. Trying to hold on to the past doesn't honor it; it sours it. You can end up making your loss the focus of your existence, rather than a waypoint on the journey.

We've talked a lot about the validity of grief, so I hope you can hear my heart in this. I would be the last one to tell you exactly when your grief needs to transition to burial. That's between you and God. So ask yourself if God might be giving you a courtesy tap. Is he telling you that seasons are changing, that it's time to wind down the memorial speech and transition into the future? If not, take your time grieving. But if so, let his grace lead you forward.

You Can't Make a Map of Sorrow

To be clear, the point is not to rush through the funeral or to prematurely get over your loss. Rather, it's to keep moving. It's to respond to the seasons and stages of healing as they come.

This movement toward healing can be difficult to measure. Grief is not a linear process, after all. It doesn't take the shortest path between two points. Grief wanders. It explores. It goes back and forth, up and down. You can feel like you are finally making it out of the valley of the shadow of death one day, only to find yourself right back in it the next.

The point, though, is that healthy grief keeps moving. It doesn't refuse to move past loss, but rather it works on navigating loss, even if progress is painfully slow.

After his wife passed away, author C. S. Lewis wrote a small book called *A Grief Observed*. In it, he said, "I thought I could describe a *state*; make a map of sorrow. Sorrow, however, turns out to be not a state but a process. It needs not a map but a history."[1] That idea of history speaks of story. Of experience. Of living. In other words, you can't control or predict the grief journey; you can only experience it.

Have you ever driven over a high mountain pass and, from the top, glimpsed the countryside far below, spread out before you like a miniature world? You can see houses and fields and maybe even a town, and you know you're getting a glimpse of where the road is taking you. It feels so close, like you'll be there any minute.

You keep driving, and the panorama disappears as the road leads you back into the thick forest that covers the mountainside. You descend the mountain for what seems like forever, navigating hairpin curves and skirting more ravines and cliffs than you can count. Once in a while, you catch another glimpse of the countryside through the trees, but it doesn't seem to be getting much closer. You start to wonder if you'll ever reach the bottom. How much longer could it be? How much farther down do you have to go?

Eventually, after driving for much longer than you expected, you emerge from the woods and find yourself in the wide-open expanse you glimpsed from above. If you look backward, the mountain range you just crossed is fading into the distance. It doesn't even look that high anymore. But you know it is. You've been there, you've experienced it, and now you're on the other side.

Grieving can feel like that mountain road. You can catch periodic glimpses of joy ahead, only to be plunged back into the dark forest of doubt, pain, and loss. You feel like you're making some progress, but it's maddeningly inefficient: there are switchbacks, potholes, gravel roads, and a few wrong turns along the way.

That's okay. You'll get through the forest if you just keep moving. You don't have to carve a road in the forest—God has that part figured out. You just have to keep moving. That's your job. Trust the road. Trust God's grace that sustains and leads you.

By the way, switchbacks on mountain roads are important. If they weren't there, the road would be too steep, and you might lose control. In the same way, healing is gradual, one level and layer at a time. As you walk through your death experiences, let healing do its slow, thorough, layered work.

Yes, the road is long. The journey toward healing is slow because grief is a big deal. You can't expect to get over heartbreak in a day.

Don't put healing on a timetable. Or rather, don't put it on your timetable. Instead, look and listen for God's timing.

Do you need to move forward today? If so, God's grace is there for you. He'll lead you through the forests and the valleys, through the stinging disappointments and the crushing losses. Listen for his voice. Pay attention to his gentle courtesy taps, nudging you along. If you keep going, you'll make it through.

SEVENTEEN

Unsinkable You

My family has always been into cruising, and I've probably sailed on forty different cruises in my life. One in particular stands out, though: an Alaskan cruise. I remember it like it was yesterday. It was summertime, which meant the days were long—something like eighteen consecutive hours of sunlight, which is enough to mess with your sleep habits. But that wasn't the worst part. My little sister had just seen the movie *Titanic*, which was terrible timing, considering we were going to Alaska. She had convinced herself that we were going to hit an iceberg and sink.

The ship journeyed farther and farther north. One morning the captain's voice came over the loudspeakers. He told passengers to look out their windows because we were surrounded by massive glaciers and icebergs. To our surprise, the ship began to hit some of the icebergs, causing one loud crash after another. I looked at my sister, and by this time she had turned blue at the thought of our ship sinking like a lead ball.

What she didn't know, however, was that there was a distinct difference between the *Titanic* and our Alaskan cruise ship. The

Titanic wasn't built for impact. Our ship was. It had been designed to navigate rough, ice-filled waters.

We survived, of course. My sister got over her trauma eventually, and the cruise itself was beautiful—I highly recommend it. Just make sure you're on a ship that is built for the trip.

You know what else I recommend? Having an unsinkable *soul*. A soul that is built to withstand the storms and impacts of life. By "storms," I don't just mean the trials and tribulations we face. I mean the emotional storms that assail us. I mean the waves of fear, the winds of sorrow, and a few icebergs of panic floating here and there.

You see, death experiences can make you feel like you're on a boat adrift in choppy, dangerous, stormy seas. The security of the familiar shoreline is gone, and you find yourself navigating waves of pain and loss. You long for the safety of the harbor, the life you used to know, but you're a long way from land. You feel alone, confused, unsafe, tossed around by life.

I don't mean to sound overly dramatic, but we've probably all felt this way at times. Maybe you are dealing with the loss of a job, or you were recently diagnosed with a chronic illness, or you had to drop out of school and put your education on hold. Whatever difficult experience you might be facing, your *loss* can make you feel *lost*. Your pain can make you feel like nothing around you is stable, secure, or safe.

Depending on what you have lost, it could take weeks or months to find stability, a new normal of sorts. Even then, you might have to deal with some of the ongoing effects of the loss for years to come, not to mention the periodic waves of sorrow that show up out of the blue. This means that the emotions and sensations of being adrift in a storm could be with you for a while.

You can't control the storms of loss or predict the sailing time of grief, at least not completely. But that doesn't mean you have to live in panic. It doesn't mean you have to be at the mercy of time, chance, and emotion. And it definitely doesn't mean your soul has to sink. Instead, you can be wise about how you navigate during difficult times. Just like a sailor at sea has equipment designed specifically for rough weather, you have access to spiritual and emotional tools that will see you through these storms of grief and loss.

What are these things? Faith. Courage. Hope. Wisdom. Grit. Peace. Self-control. Coffee. Those are the first ones that spring to mind, but there are more.

For now, though, I want to focus on one particular tool that will serve you well in any storm. As a matter of fact, this one is so versatile and effective that I would rank it as more important than anything on the list above. Even coffee.

It is love.

Love and Be Loved

Now, love might not be the first thing that comes to mind when you think about having an unsinkable soul during storms of death and sorrow. It might seem more logical to pick up tools like faith or courage or peace. Those will certainly help, so by all means use them too.

But love deserves special attention. Love, in my opinion, is one of the most effective ways to find stability and strength when we are going through pain, yet it's one of the easiest to overlook. Storms scream for our attention, so we tend to shut out everyone and everything else in the name of survival.

I've noticed that pain, loss, and grief have an almost overwhelming "me effect." That is, when I'm hurting, I think about me, I watch out for me, I feel bad for me, I spoil me, I cater to me, I talk about me. I see everything through the filter of me.

That's probably normal and fine—for a bit. (That word *bit* is intentionally vague because I have no idea what you might be suffering, so I can't pretend to know how long that feeling should or will last.) But eventually, probably sooner rather than later, you need to begin to see beyond your own feelings and pain. If your whole world orbits *you*, that is a small world indeed. Don't let pain shrink you like that. Don't allow loss and disappointment to isolate you.

This is where love comes in. Love reminds you that you are not alone. It pulls you out of your own head, your own heart, your own hurt. It keeps you from sinking by reminding you that you are both loved and called to love.

Love is such a strong, trustworthy force because it comes from God himself. John wrote, "Dear friends, let us love one another, for love comes from God. Everyone who loves has been born of God and knows God. Whoever does not love does not know God, because God is love" (1 John 4:7–8). A couple of verses later, he added, "This is love: not that we loved God, but that he loved us and sent his Son as an atoning sacrifice for our sins" (v. 10).

John was reminding us that the reason we can love one another is that God is love, and God loved us first. In times of death and loss, those are important truths to embrace. Before you focus on loving people, let God love you. That might be all you are able to do for quite some time after a loss, and that's okay. His love will strengthen and heal you. Let love do its work. You have nothing to prove, nothing to earn, nothing to hide. Hide yourself and find yourself in God's infinite love.

> **Before you focus on loving people, let God love you.**

Something happens when you begin to be filled with God's love. Not only does it change you and heal you, but it also flows out of you. Soon you can hardly tell where "being loved by God" stops and "loving your neighbor" starts. You know you are loved, and you know the same God who loves you loves everyone around you. So how could you not love them too? This outflow of love keeps you upright and stable—or at least relatively so—even when the world around you feels like a raging sea.

Love doesn't make the pain go away, though. If you are going through a nasty breakup with someone you thought was the love of your life but turned out to be a liar and a cheater, I'm not saying you can make the hurt go away by baking cookies for a neighbor or buying coffee for the person behind you at Starbucks. They'll feel the love, I'm sure, and their happiness will probably rub off on you a bit, but you'll still feel the sting of loss and death. You'll still feel like taking a baseball bat to your ex-lover's car or at least deleting every picture of them from your social media.

Although love can't magically erase your pain, it does change your perspective and your experience of pain. Instead of being paralyzed by it, you walk through it. Instead of being overwhelmed by it, you overcome it. Instead of being isolated by it, you become bigger and more generous through it. When you allow yourself to love and be loved, you rebuild the human connections that pain tried to sever. That doesn't just benefit you; it benefits everyone you are connected to.

Love Will Carry You Through the Storm

How exactly does love help you when you're caught in the crazy storms that death experiences create? Where does love fit into the emotions that overwhelm your heart? How can love guide your thoughts and decisions as you reimagine a future you never asked for? How can love keep your soul from sinking?

Going back to the boat-in-a-storm metaphor, let's talk about four ways that love will help you survive—and even keep you moving forward—in times of hurt, loss, and disappointment.

Love is an anchor.

In shallow water, an anchor digs into the seafloor and keeps the boat from drifting. In deeper water, there are special kinds of anchors that keep the boat from drifting fast or being broadsided by a wave.

Love has a similar function. It keeps you still and grounded, even when winds and waves are raging around you. Maybe your heart and mind are all over the place right now. You feel everything at once, you have a million ideas a minute, and everything is bigger than life. That can be exhausting, even overwhelming. In the middle of all the chaos, love is a grounding point. It attaches you to the only thing that is truly immovable: God himself.

If you're feeling overwhelmed right now, give this a try. Focus on God's love for you for a couple of minutes, allowing his acceptance and approval to give you peace. Remind yourself that even if all else fails, you still have God. You still have heaven. You still have his love.

Then begin to think of people close to you. Set aside your own hurt (not permanently, but just for a moment) and ask yourself what it would look like to love those people more today. Can you help them? Can you serve them? Can you encourage them?

Let your perspective shift and your posture relax. If you can love, you'll be okay.

Love is a radio.

I've never figured out why, in so many movies, the boat's radio always seems to break down right when it's most needed. Radios have one job—to communicate. Yet they always seem to go on the blink exactly when some poor captain has lost all engine power and is drifting into the path of the biggest storm the planet has ever known. (Cue dramatic music.)

In real life, if I were sailing anywhere close to a storm, the last thing I would want is to find myself cut off from the outside world. That's why I'd probably pack an extra radio, or a satellite phone, or whatever tech exists to communicate with the nonaquatic world.

Like a radio, love is a point of contact with the outside world. It opens up communication with other people, which is a vital part of surviving the storms of life. You don't have to face loss and hurt alone. You can engage love and call for help.

Engage the *love of God* in prayer, faith, trust, and patience. Engage the *love of others* by reaching out to friends, finding trusted people to talk to, and getting good advice rather than just making wild decisions. Engage *your own love* by being generous and kind even when your own pain is still raw and real. Everyone is hurting in some way, after all; if we love, we help one another heal.

Love doesn't break down when you need it most, like a radio in an overly epic adventure film. It's always there, ready to connect you and surround you.

Love is a compass.

The point of a compass is to show you which direction is north. Theoretically, if you know where north is, you should be able to get where you're going. For most of us, though, north means absolutely nothing. If we didn't have GPS and maps on our phones, with moving blue dots showing us our current location, we'd be in trouble.

Love, like a compass, points you in the right direction. That doesn't mean it's easy to get to where you want to go, but at least you have a goal, a bearing, a direction to aim for.

Let me explain. When things are going well, it's easy to get off course. If your income is skyrocketing, for example, you might find safety in the number of digits in your bank-account balance. But what happens if you lose that income? First, you freak out. But eventually, you reevaluate. You remind yourself that money is not as solid or as satisfying as you thought. It's important, and you need to be wise about it—but it's not a trustworthy compass to orient your life direction.

On the other hand, if you are in great pain, you can also lose your bearings. As I mentioned earlier, pain can make you focus inward, on yourself, as you attempt to survive. That's not a good long-term goal, though. Sure, you need to survive. But life is about more than just not dying. That's setting a very low bar. You need something that points you past the pain that fills your vision.

Love keeps you headed in the right direction. You'll make it through the confusion and chaos, the wind and waves. Love won't turn out to be an illusion or a false friend. It won't let you click into survivor mode. In good times or bad, if you aim toward love, you'll find your way.

Love is a helm.

A compass tells you which direction the boat needs to go, but the helm is what you use to actually steer the boat. It's the wheel that moves the rudder one way or another as you make your way through the waves.

In the same way, not only does love give you a long-term goal to orient your life by, but it helps you make the day-to-day course corrections you need to get there.

This is particularly important when you're reeling from pain and loss. Don't make random, rash decisions. Don't panic and do the first thing that pops into your head. Don't let a survival-mode mentality take you down the path of least resistance.

Instead, before you act or speak, engage love. Consult love. Sit with love. Think about God's love and value for you; think about loved ones who are there for you; think about how you can act in love.

You'll find it easier not to make confusing choices if you let love steer the boat.

Storms Come and Storms Go

In times of loss and pain, the storm can seem intense, scary, loud. But here's the thing with storms: They don't stick around forever. Sooner or later they blow over.

If you're currently going through the kind of emotional or mental storm that often follows death experiences, take heart. This storm won't last either. Eventually the sky will clear. The wind will die down. The waves will become gentle. You might feel that you're adrift now, but let love be your anchor, your radio, your compass, your helm. You'll find safe harbor once more.

In the meantime, don't let the storm replace your peace with fear. In retrospect, it was a terrible idea for my sister to watch *Titanic* prior to a cruise. Why? Because it exaggerated the threat and undermined her confidence in our ship. However, our ship was designed to do precisely what it was doing—navigate rough waters safely—and the result (for those of us who actually opened our eyes) was the most breathtaking view imaginable.

In the same way, turn your focus from the wind and the waves and to Jesus, the one who created your soul and keeps you afloat no

Keep your faith in Jesus, trust your unsinkable soul—and enjoy the view.

matter what. Instead of imagining the worst, believe for the best. You, too, were built to withstand storms. Like that Alaskan cruise ship, you are tough, solid, and designed to last. Keep your faith in Jesus, trust your unsinkable soul—and enjoy the view.

EIGHTEEN

Mistakes Were Made

Have you ever been to a funeral where the deceased person was (to put it delicately) a little bit "complicated"? I'm talking about someone whose personal issues or personality traits were so obvious, and often so toxic, that they had a reputation with those who knew them.

I've officiated a few funerals like this, and they are not easy. Part of my brain knows the person is no longer present, so they aren't going to get their feelings hurt no matter what I say. Another part of my brain knows their loved ones and friends are grieving, and even though they might have mixed emotions, it's pointless and almost disrespectful to bring up mistakes of the past. A third part of my brain knows that everybody is aware of the dark side of this person, and it feels dishonest to praise them without acknowledging the pain they caused, particularly if the people they hurt are in the room.

There's another complicating factor in this sort of funeral, and maybe you've felt it as well. Often the loved ones who are left behind feel a sense of guilt that they weren't closer to this person, that they didn't spend more time together or do more to help. So while the minister is trying to give the eulogy without saying too much or too little, they're seated in the front row wrestling with their own complex feelings and bittersweet memories.

Like I said, it's not easy.

Here's the thing: Eulogies are complicated because *people* are complicated. Not just the few whose mistakes were made in public and whose reputations precede them, but all people. Each of us has our share of failures and successes. We all hurt and get hurt. We all love and are loved. We all give and take, build and break, harm and heal.

It's because of this complexity that funerals are often not only a time to say goodbye but a time to forgive. To forgive the deceased, of course, but also to forgive yourself. Sins, hurts, mistakes, and weaknesses are acknowledged and then buried, even though healing might still take some time.

What does all this have to do with our death experiences? With our "little deaths," as we've called them? Simply this: when we lose something, our grieving process often needs to include *forgiveness*.

Whether we are mourning the loss of people, dreams, security, or something else, that loss is probably a mix of good and bad. Mistakes were made. There were parts of that thing that helped us, and there were parts that hurt us. That creates mixed feelings and bittersweet memories.

Too often we try to rush through a loss without sitting with its complexity. We discussed this earlier when we looked at the concept of nuance. Either we want to idolize and idealize whatever it was or we want to demonize and vilify it. Both are overly simplistic.

Instead, we need to make room for healing: first, by acknowledging both the good and the bad; and second, by embracing forgiveness. Whether the hurt was caused by a person, by adverse circumstances, by our own mistakes, or by something else, it is real and needs to be released. We can't carry blame and bitterness toward anyone—others or ourselves—for the rest of our lives. We weren't built for that and we weren't meant for that.

Toxic Forgiveness Is Not Forgiveness at All

Before we look at how forgiveness can help us deal with loss, pain, or disappointment, we need to realize that not everything we call forgiveness is actually forgiveness. Sometimes it's denial. Sometimes it's gaslighting. Sometimes it's insecurity. Sometimes it's fear of confrontation. Sometimes it's emotional abuse.

Forgiveness must be voluntary or it's not forgiveness at all. That is, if a death experience you are walking through left behind some scars, it's your *choice* to forgive. It's also your choice how to respond afterward, what limits to draw, and how long the process will take. I'm a firm believer that forgiveness is meant to restore autonomy, not take it away.

Too often we don't know what forgiveness means. Forgiveness does *not* mean you don't feel hurt anymore. It does *not* mean you can't seek justice. It does *not* mean you stay in a harmful, abusive environment. It does *not* mean there are no consequences for harm done to you. It does *not* mean you have to stay silent. It does *not* mean you must act like nothing happened. And it does *not* mean you have to "get over it" on somebody else's timetable.

Forgiveness is messier than that, which is why it often makes people uncomfortable. Forgiveness is a process, one that takes place more on the inside than the outside, and it's unique to each person and each situation.

When it comes to going through loss, sometimes we just want to move on, so we sweep the good, the bad, and the ugly under the rug of forgetfulness: "It's over now, it's done, and I don't want to think about it anymore." But we do. We wake up thinking about how we were hurt. We go to sleep trying to forget the ways we were damaged. Random conversations or things we see on social media trigger us, taking us right back to that loss.

If a loss is big enough to wake you up, keep you up, or tear you up, it's important enough to process. Don't ignore the bad things that were done to you in the name of forgiveness, and don't gaslight yourself in an effort to avoid more pain. Sure, you have to take the bad with the good—but don't call the bad good. That doesn't help anybody.

> **If a loss is big enough to wake you up, keep you up, or tear you up, it's important enough to process.**

Instead, be honest about what you've lost. Recognize that for whatever reason, mistakes were made, and they wreaked havoc in your world. Mourn the loss of the good things you used to enjoy and mourn the suffering from the bad things that came with it. Mourn mistakes you made and mistakes others made. Mourn the harm that happened, no matter who caused it or why. Take the time you need to sort through the complexities of it all.

Then, and only then, can you truly let it go.

Am I in the Place of God?

Remember the story of Joseph that we looked at earlier when we were talking about dreams? Not only is Joseph an example of how to survive the death of a dream; he's also an example of how to forgive. Notice his mature, nuanced perspective at the end of the story.

When Joseph's brothers saw that their father was dead, they said, "What if Joseph holds a grudge against us and pays us back for all the wrongs we did to him?" So they sent word to Joseph, saying, "Your father left these instructions before he died: 'This is what you are to say to Joseph: I ask you to forgive your brothers the sins and the wrongs they committed in treating you so badly.' Now please forgive the sins of the servants of the God of your father." When their message came to him, Joseph wept.

His brothers then came and threw themselves down before him. "We are your slaves," they said.

But Joseph said to them, "Don't be afraid. Am I in the place of God? You intended to harm me, but God intended it for good to accomplish what is now being done, the saving of many lives. So then, don't be afraid. I will provide for you and your children." And he reassured them and spoke kindly to them. (Genesis 50:15–21)

There's a lot going on in this passage, including an understandable level of fear and guilt among the brothers. What stands out the most to me, however, is the little phrase Joseph used to explain his mindset: "Am I in the place of God?"

In other words, Joseph wouldn't kill them because that wasn't his place. He recognized God's grace and sovereignty in the entire ordeal. Of course, his brothers shouldn't have sold him into slavery. They knew that and Joseph knew it. But Joseph could see the bigger picture. He realized they were all under the umbrella of God's sovereignty, and even the bad things could work together for good.

I wonder how long it took Joseph to reach that point. I doubt it happened overnight. My guess is he spent a lot of time wrestling with the loss, pain, disappointment, and betrayal he had suffered. Eventually, though, he must have realized he didn't have to play God.

That understanding is an important part of the forgiveness

process. It might be the most important part, actually. When you realize that your loss, hurt, and pain are safer in God's hands than yours, you can stop playing God. That means releasing your need for control or vengeance. When you do, you can begin to see God's hand at work bringing good out of evil.

This does not mean you can't fight for justice, change, repentance, or reparation. It simply means you aren't fighting for revenge. You aren't naming yourself the judge, jury, and executioner for everybody who has ever hurt you. How exhausting would that be, anyway?

This principle of not being "in the place of God" will look different depending on the death experience you're dealing with. If it was a person who hurt you, then forgiveness will probably look a bit like Joseph: you might be honest, sad, angry, and direct—but you don't have to be vindicative.

But what if your funeral has nothing to do with being hurt by a person? Maybe the economy changed and your business crumbled. Maybe an illness or tragedy struck your family. Maybe you made a mistake, and all the blame lies with you. In these cases, getting revenge isn't really an option because there's nobody to go after anyway. So what does forgiveness look like?

> **Trust that the evil things can ultimately work for good because that's what God does.**

I think it looks like letting God be God and not trying to play his role. There is a lot we won't understand until we get to heaven, and obsessing over things beyond our pay grade requires having a bit of a God complex. You don't always have to decide whom to blame for what. Release the control, the blame, the shame, the regret.

Trust that the evil things can ultimately work for good because that's what God does.

Joseph's question was rhetorical. "Am I in the place of God?" No, of course not. That went without saying—but I think Joseph said it anyway to remind his brothers that they weren't either. Maybe also to keep himself from absolutely losing it on his brothers, since he was just as human as you and I.

Yes, mistakes were made in his past. Big ones. Mean, harmful, horrible, intentional ones. But God was still in control. Joseph was able to hold both of those truths at once, and it set him free.

Unfortunately, we aren't always as self-aware as Joseph, so we might need to ask ourselves the same question a little more literally. *Am I in the place of God? Am I trying to know what only God can know? Am I seeking revenge for something only God should handle? Am I holding on to an expectation that needs to die because I can't believe God has a better plan? Have I decided that the future is hopeless, or the present is depressing, or the past is tragic, all based on my limited perspective?*

If you answered yes to any of those questions, remind yourself that it's okay to let go of the things you shouldn't be carrying in the first place. That's not called irresponsibility or weakness. It's called humility.

It's also called faith, I might add. It takes faith to forgive, because when you let go of the stuff you were clinging to, you have to trust that God is going to take care of it.

What mistakes were made in your life, either by you or others? Are you hurt by the past? Has a death experience left you in pain? As I've said before, take the time you need to grieve. Nobody blames you for that. But sooner or later, move on to forgiveness. Forgive other people. Forgive yourself. Forgive God if you're mad at him. Forgive life and luck and the economy and anything else that has caused you pain.

Then—bury that thing. Let it go. Leave it behind. You don't

have to forget about it any more than you would forget about a loved one who passed away. But don't carry the wounds or guilt or regret any longer.

Let God be God. He's pretty good at it.

Part III: Eulogy

QUESTIONS FOR REFLECTION

Chapter 13. Shades of Blue

1. Have you ever been both sad and happy about a life change? Were those emotions confusing? How did you handle that?
2. Why is it important to recognize both the good and the bad in the things we lose?
3. Can you think of a time when God brought life out of a difficult situation for you—that is, where you experienced loss or pain, but good somehow came from it? How did the good that came from it end up affecting the way you originally viewed the bad?

Chapter 14. Ice Baths for the Soul

1. Do you consider yourself good at handling pain? What are some kinds of pain (whether physical or emotional) that are more difficult for you to deal with?

2. When you are going through a difficult experience, such as a loss, tragedy, or disappointment, how do you respond to the pain? What advice would you give someone else who is going through pain?

3. Can you think of any benefits that pain brings? Explain.

Chapter 15. Surfing Monsters

1. Are you good at managing your emotions? What are some ways you need to improve when it comes to how you deal with strong feelings such as anger, fear, offense, or hurt?

2. What strategies have you found that help you manage strong emotions in difficult moments?

3. When you are feeling overwhelmed by a particular emotion or situation, does your relationship with God help you regain your peace and stability? In what ways does your faith in God influence your emotions?

Chapter 16. Let Go of the Mic

1. Have you ever found yourself in a prolonged period of grief? Was it healthy or unhealthy to grieve for that length of time? How did you eventually move on?

2. Based on your own experiences going through difficult times, what are the best ways to help or comfort someone who is grieving?

3. How do you think God responds to our sorrow? How does your relationship with God help you walk through sorrow and come out on the other side?

Chapter 17. Unsinkable You

1. Have you ever been in a season of grief or pain that was so hard you didn't know how you would survive? How did that make you feel? How did you work through it?

2. In what ways can love help you navigate circumstances that are threatening or confusing?

3. Besides love, what are some other values that can help you keep your head above water and make good decisions in difficult moments?

Chapter 18. Mistakes Were Made

1. Would you consider yourself someone who forgives quickly or who tends to hold on to a grudge? Do you think you need to adjust toward one direction or the other? What makes you say that?

2. Have you ever been told to forgive in a way that you felt wasn't wise or right (that is, toxic forgiveness)? Were you eventually able to forgive whatever it was that happened? If so, what did forgiveness look like for you (if it's not too personal)?

3. What does the example of Joseph tell you about forgiveness and about God's purposes and plans? Are there any areas of your life where you need to forgive a person or circumstance and allow God to turn that evil into good?

PART IV

Recessional

Closure

After the minister has led the congregation in honoring their loved one, the funeral draws to a close. It ends with a simple recessional as the pallbearers carry the casket to a waiting hearse.

This is a moment of solemn finality, but also one of closure. A life has been honored, remembered, celebrated. Now the family and friends of the deceased must move forward into a new kind of future. They will miss their loved one, but they know they can't stay in the church or at the graveside forever. They must end the funeral and restart their lives.

When the minister finishes the eulogy, the air is charged with emotion. The family in the front row is wiping their eyes, but they have a look of peace and calm. Most of the congregation, even those who didn't know the deceased very well, are moved.

It's not possible to summarize a life in a few minutes. Not even close. But what is clear is that life is full, complex, and beautiful.

The pastor leads a final prayer as the funeral draws to a close. There has been a subtle shift in the room from the past to the future, from death to life. The grief is still real, and it won't go away soon. But there is a degree of closure now. A life has been lived, celebrated, and honored. The deceased made a difference; their absence leaves a loss. They will be remembered by the loved ones who remain.

Next, the recessional. The pastor again leads the way. The pallbearers walk behind him, carrying the casket down the aisle, followed in turn by the family. The church doors open and daylight floods the sanctuary once more. The yellow light, the rush of summer humidity, and the chirping of birds in the trees are simple reminders that the world is still here. Nothing has changed, even though everything has changed.

The casket is placed in the hearse and the procession to the cemetery begins. It's an impressive sight: vehicle after vehicle, headlights on, hazard lights flashing, forming a line that winds slowly toward the deceased's final resting place. Other drivers pull over out of respect. Finally, the graveside ceremony: a short service followed by tears and embraces.

Afterward, family and friends gather for a reception, where they eat together, remembering and celebrating their loved one. They reminisce about the past and simultaneously look to the future. A life is over, but life itself continues. Death is not the end because love cannot be buried in a grave.

This is death, and this is life, and this is love.

It's difficult to imagine anything more final than death, yet death is not the end. Not for those who are still living, that is. That is why, after the funeral, they must make peace with their loss and move forward into the future. They must find closure.

In our death experiences—our losses, our disappointments, our pain—we need to find closure as well. We need to make peace with the past while simultaneously stepping into the future. This includes finding *peace*, developing *gratitude*, embracing *hope*, leaning into *growth*, being surprised by *joy*, and ultimately *moving on*. Without dismissing the pain of the present, we must begin to look toward the future. After all, grief and hope go hand in hand. And even in death, God brings life.

NINETEEN

Sweet Tea and Inner Peace

I grew up in North Carolina. Not in Charlotte, which is what most people think of when they hear "North Carolina," but in a rural part of the state. As in, the country. The backwater. The sticks.

Back then, out in the country, they made sweat tea. I'm not talking about the city version of sweet tea either. This was *real* sweet tea, the kind where after one sip, you needed dialysis. I remember my mom making tea every week in a small trash can that was used just for that purpose. It was fifteen gallons of pure, sugary happiness.

Sometimes I would walk into the kitchen during the process, and I'd see all these tea bags soaking in the water, extracting the flavor. Once that step was finished, she'd remove the tea bags, pour the tea into the container, and then add all the sugar. More than once, I tried to sneak some of the tea when she wasn't looking. The problem was, the sugar hadn't dissolved into the tea yet, so it tasted terrible. My mom would laugh at me and say, "The sugar is all at the bottom. It's gonna be bitter until you stir it up."

The bitterness meant the sugar needed to be mixed in. It had to be stirred. It had to be disrupted. My mom would grab a wooden spoon and vigorously stir the tea until all that sweetness had swirled up into the liquid and changed its flavor.

The disruptions and the stirring in your life are accomplishing something similar. The little deaths, the losses, the pain, the confusion—those difficult moments have a way of reaching deep into your soul and bringing the sweetness of God to the surface. I know it doesn't feel like it in the moment, because disruption is never comfortable. But God has placed things inside you that he wants to stir up, things that will replace bitterness with sweetness, that will give flavor to your character, your relationships, and your actions.

Without the disruption, there is no flavor. Just bitterness. It's the deep work of God in your soul—often through uncomfortable, painful experiences—that gives you sweetness and enhances your flavor. That doesn't always mean the hard things make sense, of course, but it does give them a redeeming element. You aren't suffering in vain. Instead, your pain is making you better, sweeter, kinder, more patient, and more mature.

Rather than resisting the stirring that is happening, that disruption of your inner world, you need to come to a place of inner peace. Let God do his work of stirring, of sweetening, and of settling. Regardless of whose fault the loss was, the healing will come from him.

Inner peace is connected to acceptance. Just as a funeral ends with the recessional and burial, so the seasons of grief in our lives are eventually laid to rest, and we begin to adjust to a new reality. Our little deaths, those things we have lost, are receding from view, like the casket at a funeral, and we are saying our final goodbyes. We can't go back to the way things were before, but we don't have to. Even though the future will be different, it will be good in its own way.

Again, I want to emphasize that there is no one-size-fits-all pattern to walking through death experiences, so I'm not going to tell you how you should or shouldn't be grieving. I don't even need to. Our bodies and minds instinctively know how to grieve, and we mostly just need to let grief run its course. We should be wise and emotionally intelligent while that happens, of course, so that we don't hurt ourselves or anyone around us. But grief is natural. Tears are going to flow with or without our permission. Our hearts will break at times because that's what hearts do.

Do you know what else is natural? *Healing.* Hearts don't just break; they also mend. Our bodies don't just know how to mourn; they know how to find happiness and joy again. So not only do we need to get out of the way of our grief; we also need to get out of the way of our healing. We can't keep fighting for a past we will never regain, because if we do, we are resisting the grieving and healing process itself.

Grief eventually leads to peace. Mourning is ultimately turned into joy. It's part of the process. Remember the five stages of grief that psychiatrist Elisabeth Kübler-Ross defined? They are denial, anger, bargaining, depression, and acceptance. While these can happen in any order, the last one—acceptance—is where you ultimately must land.

Find Your Peace Through Acceptance

One of the most important steps toward closure is acceptance of loss. By *acceptance*, I don't mean just saying, "Yes, this bad thing happened." That is assent, but it's not necessarily acceptance. I also don't mean saying, "This is terrible, I'll never recover, so I'll just get used to living with pain." That is giving up, not acceptance. By acceptance, I mean something deeper and more difficult to measure: an *inner* acceptance. An emotional, mental, and even spiritual decision to make peace with our loss and to make the most of our future.

Of course, *acceptance* doesn't sound very strong or bold or exciting. It sounds weak and passive. Like we lost something or failed at something. We're told our whole lives not to give up or give in. We're taught to fight for what we want; to be conquerors, not victims. Maybe that's why our initial reactions in the face of death experiences are usually a lot more aggressive: fighting, yelling, denying, arguing, bargaining, and pleading. Nobody wants to go down without a fight.

I get that. I'm like that too. I think it's human nature to fight until we have exhausted every option. There is nothing wrong with refusing to give up easily—it's proof that we care deeply.

The problem, though, is that it's hard to know where the line is. For example, if you find out you are about to lose your job, how hard should you try to keep it? Should you talk to everyone you can? Email all your superiors? Show up early and work overtime? If you do get laid off, should you try to get your job back? See if you can negotiate a different position? Demand a better exit package? Complain about your ex-boss to their supervisor? File a wrongful termination suit?

Or maybe you're dealing with a broken relationship with a best friend. Should you call them a dozen times? Pursue them aggressively? Try to talk them into working it out? Do you give them space and let them come to you? Or do you simply decide to move on?

Or possibly you've always had a dream of having the perfect family—a spouse, kids, a family dog, a home—but your life didn't go that direction. You never got married, maybe, or you went through a divorce. When you think about the dream that now seems impossible, you feel grief and loss. So what should you do? Fast and pray? Join seventeen online dating sites? Rent a billboard with your face and phone number on it? (That seems a little sketchy.) Find a spouse, any spouse, and get started? (That's even sketchier.)

If you're expecting answers to these questions, sorry, but I'm going to disappoint you. I don't know what to do any more than you do. There is no easy-to-define line between "This is healthy resistance to loss" and "This is superweird and borderline obsessive." You have to figure that out for yourself.

By the way, figuring it out *for* yourself is not the same as figuring it out *by* yourself. If you're struggling to come to a place of acceptance, if you can't seem to make peace with the hand life dealt you, get help. Educate yourself about your situation and your loss rather than staying in limbo forever, wondering whether you should give up or keep fighting. That might be as simple as reading a book or doing some research online. It might mean finding a trusted friend who will listen for a long time and then tell you the truth, even if it hurts. It might mean going to therapy. Whatever it takes, look for ways to deal wisely with loss, whether that means refusing to accept it or choosing to accept it.

I mentioned earlier that the stages of grief are not linear. That means the goal isn't to plow through them as fast as possible, get to the acceptance stage, and magically feel better. In my experience, acceptance is not a one-time achievement, like reaching the finish line after running a marathon. If it were, then all you'd have to do is try really hard and work for a long time, and eventually you'd get there. The marathon would be forever behind you, and you'd have nothing to worry about going forward.

Grief is not like that, and neither is acceptance. Acceptance is less permanent than that. You'll find that you reach a place of relative acceptance one day, but the next day you slip back into sorrow and anger. Then you'll accept your loss again, only to be triggered by something and end up grieving once more.

That's okay. Go with it. Flow with it. Your mind and body know what they need, and they'll follow their own schedule. Don't be in a hurry to reach some "I'm over it now" place. It's not realistic, nor is it healthy.

Rather than getting over it, make peace with it. There's a difference. Getting over something implies you are no longer affected by it. You don't miss it, you don't need it, and you aren't hurting because it's gone. It sounds tough. But it's often a facade.

To make peace with a loss, on the other hand, is to recognize openly that it affected you, but it didn't destroy you and it will not stop you. It's a sort of internal truce: You decide that you will no longer be divided in your heart and mind, with one side of you knowing that the loss has happened and the other refusing to accept it. Instead, you'll look realistically and hopefully at the situation, and you'll move forward undefeated.

There's nothing shameful about acceptance. It's actually a sign of maturity and inner strength. It's an active choice, not a passive reaction. That means choosing what to accept and when to accept it is the opposite of being a victim—it's a way to reclaim your human dignity and autonomy.

Calm Down a Little

We talked earlier about Job, the poor guy in the Bible who lost just about everything he valued in a matter of days. His wife was understandably upset, and she finally snapped at Job, "Are you still maintaining your integrity? Curse God and die!" (Job 2:9).

Job's reply is fascinating. "You are talking like a foolish woman. Shall we accept good from God, and not trouble?" (v. 10). If I called my wife a foolish woman, that would be the end of me right then and there, so I'm not recommending that part of his reply. I love the second half, though: "Shall we accept good from God, and not trouble?" It's one of those rhetorical questions. Job was saying that we can't just trust God, love God, and submit to God when everything is going right. We can and must do the same even when life knocks us down. We must be able to accept things we don't like or understand.

For the next thirty-five chapters, Job and his friends debate the existence of suffering. It's written as a poem, so the guys use a lot of metaphors and hyperbole. Job mostly complains, and his friends mostly try to tell him he is at fault and needs to repent. The argument goes in circles, and nobody seems to be listening to anyone else, like some ancient version of Twitter.

Remember, this conversation took place while Job was going through incredible loss. He was suffering physical and emotional pain. I totally get why he complained as much as he did—I probably would have reacted more like his wife, to be honest.

At the end of the story, God takes four chapters to basically tell them that they are too simplistic and too human in their approach, and they all need to calm down a little and let God be God. He reminds them that he can speak for himself, but he doesn't have to explain himself. He tells them to look at the beauty, scale, and complexity of the created universe to take down their pride a notch. They can't explain or create or manage such a world, but God can. So who are they to explain God?

Interestingly, God didn't get upset with Job for grieving. He didn't shut him down or tell him to stop being a wimp. He didn't seem to mind the venting at all. What he objected to was being put in a box, which was what Job's friends were doing with their pompous explanations of what God wants, how God thinks, and whom God blesses.

At this point, Job said something else amazing: "Surely I spoke of things I did not understand, things too wonderful for me to know" (42:3). He humbly admitted his human limitations, his limited perspective and knowledge. Even in his pain—or especially in his pain—he let God be God.

After that, God restored all that Job had lost—and much more. Job probably had to deal with some deep-seated trauma for a while, but life was good again and his grieving was over.

Job is a fantastic model of acceptance because he was completely transparent with his suffering, but he was also able to release control to God. His acceptance was the natural result of recognizing God's sovereignty. He knew where the line was between what he could control and fix and what he couldn't.

We don't know how long Job's suffering lasted. It was probably months, at least. Maybe years. But it did end. That's one of the key points of the book. He persevered, he waited, he trusted. Simultaneously, he suffered, he complained, and he asked questions. Those things are not mutually exclusive.

Eventually God made it clear it was time to stop living in the past. He wanted Job to make peace with the present. That could happen only by taking on the peace of God, a peace that goes beyond human logic and understanding.

So how about you? Where are you in the grief-acceptance process? Do you still find yourself fighting for something you need to let go of or holding on to something you can't get back? Do you have voices whispering in your ear, like Job's friends, saying that if you would just do this or pray that, God would give you all you want, as if somehow your suffering were your fault? Or do you hear a voice from heaven reminding you that there is no vacancy for the job of ruler of the universe, and everybody needs to calm down just a little and let God be God?

God is still good and he's still in control.

No matter where you are, I'm not here to judge you, nor am I trying to rush you along. Mostly, I just want to remind you that God is still good and he's still in control. Keep going. Keep believing. Keep absorbing the peace of God. I truly believe that, like Job, you're going to see the goodness and blessing of God again.

TWENTY

Silver Linings

I love the sound of a good thunderstorm. Well, assuming I'm inside my house, of course. When I have a roof over my head and the windows are all shut, the roar and crash of a storm are actually soothing.

We have intense thunderstorms where I live in Florida, as does much of the South. They usually roll in during the summer months when the heat and humidity are the worst. The sky can be sunny and clear all morning long, but early in the afternoon, you'll start to see clouds forming on the horizon. They start small and they have a specific shape, like white bubbles squished together. Within an hour or two, they grow bigger and bigger until eventually they fill the sky.

Then, in an instant, the rain starts: a torrential downpour that will soak you to the bone in five seconds if you're caught outside. Lightning bolts and the deafening crash of thunder make you think the apocalypse has come and you are doomed. Sometimes there is hail thrown into the mix for good measure.

And then, as suddenly as it began, it's over. The rain shuts off like a faucet and the lightning stops. For a while you can still hear thunder rumbling in the distance, but even that fades eventually. The sun breaks through, lighting up the clouds from behind and creating that famous, glowing silver edge.

Even the darkest of clouds has a silver lining when the sun illuminates it. And even the darkest loss has a silver lining when God's grace shines into it.

Earlier we talked about how pain makes it difficult to see anything else. When you're hurting, you just want relief. When you've lost something invaluable, you just wish you had it back. For a while, at least, you aren't usually thinking about anything beyond survival.

Pain tends to fade with time, though. Not quickly, and maybe not totally, but things do get better. Like a broken leg, the initial sharp pain becomes more of an underlying ache as healing slowly occurs.

As the pain of a death experience becomes more manageable, you start to get a clearer perspective on what you've lost or what has changed. You also gain a more realistic understanding of what lies ahead, so you can say your final goodbyes to the loss and begin to look at life with fresh eyes.

At this point, something surprising often starts to surface in your soul: gratitude.

Gratitude might be one of the last things you expect at a funeral, but it's common, and it's also incredibly healing. Expressing the good things we have received allows us to deal with the bad ones. Even the long-winded uncle I mentioned earlier took time to talk about what he appreciated about the deceased. Too much time, of course, but at least that part of his speech was on topic.

It's the whole silver-lining-in-the-cloud thing. Maybe you lost a job you loved, but now doors are opening—better doors, even—that you wouldn't have noticed if you were still in your old role. Maybe you lost a relationship, but you feel grateful for what the person gave you and for the time you spent together, and you know that God has something better in mind for both of you.

Even though the pain is still there, you find yourself feeling grateful for the good things you had, for as long as you had them. You appreciate the goodness of God, especially in the middle of pain. You are thankful, even excited, for the opportunities and horizons ahead.

It's a cycle that pushes you upward and forward: As your pain decreases and your perspective expands, gratitude starts to bubble up. Then, as you focus on what you're grateful for, you are better able to process pain and gain perspective, which creates even more gratitude, joy, and peace. And so on.

I'm not saying it's easy or that it happens overnight, and you do have to work at it a little bit. But you would also have to work at staying permanently angry, depressed, and bitter, if you were to choose that route. Gratitude and self-pity are both choices, and they both require that you set aside some things and focus on others.

Grief and Gratitude Go Together

Before we talk more about how gratitude helps you grieve, process, and heal, let me clarify a couple of things that gratitude is not.

First, gratitude is not masochism. We are not talking about some weird martyrdom mentality where you think you are obligated to enjoy suffering. Nobody in the Bible enjoyed suffering: not Job, not Jesus, not Paul, not anyone. It's okay to hate death and be upset when you go through tough times.

Now, James did write, "Consider it pure joy, my brothers and sisters, whenever you face trials of many kinds, because you know that the testing of your faith produces perseverance" (James 1:2–3). However, he was not literally saying you have to enjoy pain. If you read the context, he was saying to be glad because the suffering you go through will build character. It was his version of "what doesn't kill you makes you stronger."

Second, gratitude is not gaslighting yourself into believing everything is fine when it's not. There is a type of toxic gratitude out there that says you should ignore the mistakes and even the abuse of people in your life because pointing out the evil that is happening would be ungrateful. Instead, they say, just focus on the good you've received and the positive things that are happening and be thankful. But why are those the only two options? I'm a strong believer that you can be grateful for the good parts of any relationship *and* work on fixing the bad parts.

What is gratitude, then? Simply put, it's the quality of being thankful or appreciative. Notice that word *quality*. It's more than just a performative "thank you." It's an inner state of being. A condition of the heart. A willingness and ability to acknowledge the good things you've been given.

> You can be grateful while you grieve, and you can grieve while you're grateful.

Gratitude doesn't mean you no longer feel pain or sorrow, though. They are not mutually exclusive emotions. You can be grateful while you grieve, and you can grieve while you're grateful.

Actually the two work well together. That's why gratitude is such a powerful tool for healing. It's healthy to think fondly of the past and to have happy memories. It helps you grieve whatever you lost, honor it, and say goodbye. It's also healthy to be glad for the new doors opening in front of you.

If you're going through a tough loss right now, I encourage you to invest a few minutes in stirring up gratitude. Again, not in a weird, forced, fake way. Gratitude isn't something you have to manufacture but rather a natural reaction that happens when you notice things that make you happy, or excited, or content, or peaceful, or encouraged. So if you want to be more thankful, think about the things you have to be thankful for. It really is that simple.

Gratitude Is Always Appropriate

What does gratitude look like when you're walking through loss? Well, it depends on the loss, and it depends on you. Like every other quality or value, you have a lot of freedom in how you express thankfulness.

Paul put it this way: "And whatever you do, whether in word or deed, do it all in the name of the Lord Jesus, giving thanks to God the Father through him" (Colossians 3:17). "Whatever" is a broad category, for sure. It doesn't get any more open-ended than that. Obviously Paul wasn't giving us some magic thankfulness formula to recite, as if God needs to be flattered or charmed before he will respond. The point isn't words, but heart. Paul was reminding us that no matter what happens, faith in Jesus and gratitude toward God are always appropriate.

In seasons of loss, pain, and disappointment, then, what are some ways to become more grateful? Based on my own experiences, conversations with others, and examples we see in the Bible, here are a few suggestions.

Give thanks for the season you enjoyed.

There's a well-known passage in Ecclesiastes that starts out, "There is a time for everything, and a season for every activity under the heavens" (3:1). From there, the author launched into a poetic list of twenty-eight seasons: to be born, to die, to plant, to uproot, to kill, to heal, to tear down, to build up, to weep, to laugh, to mourn, to dance, to scatter stones, to gather stones, to embrace, to not embrace, to search, to give up searching, to keep, to throw away, to tear, to mend, to be silent, to speak, to love, to hate, to make war, to make peace.

That's not an exhaustive list either. His point was that nothing lasts forever and everything has its time. Seasons change. That's just what they do. We can't hold on to one season for too long—it's impossible, unnatural, and harmful.

Rather than trying to freeze time, choose to be grateful for the season that has passed. Remember, there will be both good and bad within that season, so don't erase the nuances of it. No season deserves to be worshiped or despised: It simply is what it is. Or rather, it was what it was.

Now another season is starting. Give thanks for the time you spent in the last season. Then let yourself feel faith and excitement for what is ahead. God hasn't changed. If he could bless you yesterday, he can bless you today, and he will bless you tomorrow.

Give thanks for the gifts you've received.

Not only were there good moments and memories in the season that is ending, but you are a better person because of what you experienced. Be grateful for the gifts you carry with you into the next season.

These are usually intangible, but if you stop and think about it, you'll see what I mean. That person who was in your life? They left a deposit in you. You are better because of them. That job you lost? You learned something while you were there, and it will help you get better jobs in the future.

Everything works together for our good, as noted earlier; that means if you look carefully, you'll find something good that came out of every season. I can almost guarantee you that through those experiences, you have grown in your character, your maturity, your wisdom, your compassion, and your capacity. Those are gifts, my friend.

Give thanks for the challenges you overcame.

I mentioned earlier that all humans are complicated. "Mistakes were made" could be included on the epitaph for any of our lives.

The same goes for any season, any job, any dream, any opportunity, or any relationship you might have lost. Rather than feeling regret or guilt for the mistakes, try being grateful that you made it through. You probably even learned and grew through the process.

Were you perfect? Probably not. Did everything go according to plan? It's doubtful. Would you do things differently if you could? I'm sure we all would.

But you're here now. Give yourself a break and give other people a break too. Rejoice that even in the face of difficult obstacles, you came out alive. You came out ahead. You beat the odds, and that deserves celebration.

Give thanks for the God you rely on.

It's easy to forget this blessing when you're going through the valley of the shadow of death, but it's the most important of them all. God is always with you. He will never leave you, never forsake you, never forget you.

The longer I'm alive, the more grateful I am for this truth. You start to realize over time just how fleeting things like wealth, fame, titles, and power really are. But God never changes. His love never fluctuates; his mercy never runs dry. That's a truth worth hanging on to no matter what season you are in, but in times of loss and pain it's especially comforting.

Give thanks for the doors you are entering.

It's often been said that God doesn't close one door without opening another. On one hand, that's exciting because it means something new and fresh is about to happen. On the other, it's sad, because the door that was shut represented dreams and expectations that won't be fulfilled.

The question is, which door are we going to focus on—the shut door or the open one? Too often we mourn the one that was closed without realizing that if it had never slammed shut, we wouldn't have looked for another door. We were good with that first door, after all. We were comfortable with that door. We had things figured out, planned out, and under control with that door.

Then it was shut in our face, and now we're scrambling and hustling to make sense of a new reality. The scramble is normal. The hustle is good. It's called change, and change is always a little crazy.

Rather than resenting this craziness, give thanks for it. Even if *you* don't know what lies ahead (which you don't, even if you think you do), you can trust that *God* has it figured out, planned out, and under control—and that's what matters.

Watch Where Gratitude Takes You

Thank you. These two simple words can shift your perspective and help heal your soul. If you're walking through loss right now, or if you're dealing with disappointment or betrayal, take some time to whisper those words. Or, if you need something a little more tangible than a whisper, try making a list. Start by thinking about the areas I've already mentioned: the season you enjoyed, the gifts you received, the challenges you overcame, the God you rely on, and the doors you are entering. And from there, just see where gratitude takes you.

Honestly, this isn't usually an instantaneous process. I wish I could say that I always jump straight to gratitude when I go through a storm, but I don't. Usually I go through a few of the stages and emotions we've been discussing: things like anger, grief, confusion, denial, and fear. The experience is much like being caught outside during a Florida thunderstorm, when you feel like the sky itself is falling and you only hope you can make it out alive.

The storm won't last forever, though. The rain and lightning will cease. The thunder will fade into the distance. The sun will break through the canopy of dark clouds, the grace of God will illuminate your life, and the silver lining will mirror the gratitude in your soul.

Good things are on their way. You can count on it.

TWENTY-ONE

Between Fantasy and Certainty

I never play the lottery. And by "never," I mean "never, unless the lottery pool reaches a billion dollars." At that point, I figure throwing a dollar into the pool is justified. Somebody has to win, right?

A few years back, the lottery went up to about $1.4 billion. So I bought a ticket, made up five numbers, and began to dream about what I could do with my winnings. A billion dollars goes a long way, after all. The next two days were the longest of my life as I waited for the lottery drawing, which was to be held Saturday night on live television. Meanwhile, I kept imagining how much I would enjoy my winnings. I would even have been happy to split the prize with someone else if God saw fit. Seven hundred million bucks goes a long way too.

When 11:00 p.m. on Saturday rolled around, my hopes were high. I knew my odds of winning were microscopic, but that didn't stop me. The announcer began the drawing. To my utter awe and amazement, I got the first number right! I got the next one wrong, though. And the next one, and the one after that, and the last one.

I had correctly guessed one out of five numbers, which is good for exactly zero dollars in prize money.

So much for my hopes of being an instant billionaire. It ended up being a day just like every other day—but with one dollar less in my pocket.

Hope is a funny thing, isn't it? We use it for every scenario, from real possibilities to pie-in-the-sky dreams. For example:

- I hope my work meetings go well today. (Reasonably likely.)
- I hope I drive home without getting mad at anyone. (Slightly less likely but definitely possible.)
- I hope somebody else remembered to set out the garbage cans I forgot this morning. (Unlikely, but there is a remote chance.)
- I hope the Panthers win the Super Bowl this year. (Yeah, no, definitely unlikely.)
- I hope my child sleeps in on Saturday. (Humanly impossible.)
- I hope I win a billion dollars. (Not gonna happen.)

Hope is hard to define. I see it as a mix of desire and expectation that lies somewhere between fantasy and certainty. On one hand, it can't be absolute certainty, because you don't need hope if the outcome is guaranteed. On the other, it's not some fantasy. It must be at least theoretically possible—like when I had a one-in-a-bazillion chance to win the lottery. Hope hangs out in that broad, undefined place made up of wanting, needing, wishing, praying, waiting.

I've noticed that hope, like gratitude, is often present at funerals. And like gratitude, that seems surprising at first. What hope is left when a loved one is being buried?

First, there is hope of eternal life. In Jesus, death doesn't look down into the grave; it looks up toward heaven. Second, there is hope for those still present. Funerals are inspiring because we see the impact one person's life had. They spur us toward greater effort, courage, and seriousness by reminding us that tomorrow isn't guaranteed. We remember that life is full of potential, and we should make the most of it. Those future-facing desires all belong in the realm of hope.

When it comes to our death experiences, to the little deaths that are a part of life, we also have hope. First, just as with literal death, we have hope in Jesus and in heaven. Even when sorrow and loss strike on earth, we know that someday our tears will be wiped away and we will be rewarded for our faithfulness and love. Second, we have hope for the years still ahead, for the life we've been given. Death is not the end of the book, just a chapter; and we naturally hope that the pages ahead are the best part of the story.

Hope Never Dies

Hope is one of those intangible, immeasurable things we love to have but can't always figure out how to get. Like courage. Or faith. Or peace. Or sleep on Saturday mornings. We want and need hope, but sometimes it seems elusive.

Hope can be especially hard to find in times of pain and disappointment. When you've lost something important, it can feel like all that you knew to be true has turned out to be a fraud. What you thought was solid ground is quicksand. You lose hope because you've lost the source of your hope, the things you counted on to keep you safe and give you success.

I'm sure you've felt this. If you lose an important client, if you go through a severe illness, if you realize a person you trusted has been lying to you—these are all moments when hope feels lost. "They let me down," you might say, or "I was counting on that," or "I expected something different." Those are all ways of saying your hope turned out to be false. It's crushing to realize your trust was misplaced and now your dreams must pay the price.

Ironically, the moment hope seems lost is when hope works best. Why? Because hope looks for possibilities, not just proof. By definition it does not have to be logical. I don't mean it ignores logic, but it does go beyond it. When we lose one source of hope, we naturally look around for another.

It's like those inflatable, cylindrical toys with weights at the bottom designed for kids to punch. No matter how hard you hit them, they pop back up. That's how hope works. It is pretty much undefeatable. It might get knocked down, but eventually it gets back on its feet.

All hope needs is a chance and it springs to life. That's why we can hope for a last-second miracle during a football game, or we can hope to get a parking spot at Costco that is less than a half mile from the door, or we can hope our spouse will agree to an action movie tonight rather than yet another romcom. Those outcomes are not based on logic necessarily, but they exist within the realm of possibility. At least theoretically. So we keep hoping.

When you're going through loss, you need this kind of undefeatable, unkillable, unsinkable hope. A hope that gets back up even when it's been knocked down. A hope that hopes against hope.

What does death-defying hope look like? Maybe you lost your job, but you find yourself hoping for a better one. Or you lost a friend, but you're hopeful you can restore the relationship somehow or someday. Perhaps you are suffering a debilitating illness, but you're hoping to beat the odds and experience a miracle. The possibilities for hope are endless, and that's precisely my point. When your logic or emotions can't imagine good coming

Even in times of death, hope comes back to life.

out of this pain, make room for hope. Listen to its voice as it points out possibilities, opportunities, alternate futures.

Yes, in the first pangs of loss, hope seems impossible. But just wait. Give it time. You'll start to see rays of light piercing the dark clouds. Even in times of death, hope comes back to life.

I Will Yet Praise Him

Ultimately, hope should point to God. I don't mean you will never place a measure of hope in other people or even in yourself—you can and should trust people. It would be weird not to. But no human being or human endeavor is worthy of *all* your hope.

Psalms 42–43 have a lot to say about hope in times of pain and loss. These two psalms were written by songwriters who went by the title "the Sons of Korah." Their stage name sounds like a death-metal band, but their content is a lot more chill, even melancholy. These two psalms may have originally been one psalm because they repeat the same chorus:

> Why, my soul, are you downcast?
> Why so disturbed within me?
> Put your hope in God,
> for I will yet praise him,
> my Savior and my God.

(42:5, 11; 43:5)

The rest of these psalms is a lot darker. For example: "My tears have been my food day and night" (42:3), "all your waves and breakers have swept over me" (v. 7), and "my bones suffer mortal agony" (v. 10). Actually, that last line sounds like death metal too.

I don't know what life-or-death situation they were facing, but

I do know the feelings they describe. All too well. You probably do too. Sometimes it feels like all hell has broken loose and heaven is nowhere to be found. We cry during the day and we cry at night. We feel like we are drowning under waves of loss and sorrow. Our health suffers, our emotions are frayed, our sleep is affected, our joy is gone.

In the depths of grief, we can ask the same questions as the psalmist: "Why, my soul, are you downcast? Why so disturbed within me?" There are probably reasons to be sad, and good ones at that. But the next line in the chorus puts things in perspective. "Put your hope in God, for I will yet praise him, my Savior and my God." Yes, things are bad right now. But the story isn't over. We will yet praise him. We see help in the future, so we have confidence in the present. Our hearts are flooded with peace even when our lives are flooded with pain.

That is hope. Not just any hope, not your average hope, but hope *in God*. In the Creator of the universe, who also happens to be our Father and our Friend and our Savior and our God.

Recently my family and I have been going through a transition season that has included some good times as well as some traumatic, painful ones. It's been a tricky season to navigate, that's for sure. Oftentimes we're hurt not by what happens to us but rather by *what we expect not to happen* to us. We might also be hurt by *who* we did not expect to do that thing to us.

During this season I've learned—once again—to cast my expectations on Jesus. I'd strongly encourage the same for you. Give your expectations of what will and won't happen, or who will help you and who might hurt you, over to God. He is the only one capable of seeing the future. We can hope, but only God can *know*.

Here's the thing, though. Despite it being a painful season, I've seen so much of God's grace, mercy, and love. Had we not gone through this transition that was riddled with pain and chaos, we wouldn't have seen the goodness of God in the same way. He has taught us to endure by relying on the hope we have in *Jesus* rather than on merely human hopes and expectations. Even though some of our expectations proved to be wrong, our hope in Jesus is not.

If you're going through a loss, or if you've suffered a tragedy, or if you're dealing with disappointment, this hope is for you. No matter how dark it is right now, you can look toward God and find light. He is the ultimate source of possibility. If humans are so good at finding hope among the broken pieces of this flawed planet, how much more should you be able to find hope in a God who has no limits, no imperfections, no possibility of failure?

This isn't some positive-thinking pep talk. This is reality. It's a bigger reality than the one you can filter through your five senses. It's a reality that takes God into account. And honestly, that's the reality that matters most.

You might not be in a place to feel hope right now because you're still processing your loss. If so, that's okay, as I've said over and over. But hope will spring up again. I know it. I've seen it. I've felt it myself and I've watched it happen in others. After death strikes, hope rises again.

When it does, let it enter. Crack open the curtains and let the light shine in.

Will you be disappointed again? Maybe. Will you feel let down at some point? It's likely. But are you ultimately safe in God? Absolutely. Always. Without a doubt.

So today, put your hope in God. You'll praise him again very soon.

TWENTY-TWO

Grieving and Growing

At the 2021 presidential inauguration, a young Black poet named Amanda Gorman read a poem she wrote titled "The Hill We Climb." It included this powerful, honest line: "Even as we grieved, we grew."[1] She went on to talk about hoping even when we are hurting and trying even when we are tired.

The words are beautiful, but it was the *pain* and the *faith* behind them that resonated so deeply with everyone who heard her speak. The United States, like every nation, has a mixed history. I love my country, and I am grateful for the blessings that God has given us and for the influence we've had in the world. But the United States has not always been a safe place for people of color, as we all know. Even though things have improved since the days of slavery, we have a long way to go before all people—rich and poor, young and old, liberal and conservative, white and Black and brown—experience the same safety and acceptance.

That is why I love Ms. Gorman's words so much. They don't ignore the grief of the past or the struggle of the present, but they don't give up either. She recognized—as we all must—that grief is part of growth, and hurting often precedes hope, and tiredness is not a reason to quit trying. Although she was talking about the pain of a nation, the description applies to all kinds of pain and loss.

We grieve and grow; we hurt and hope; we get tired and keep trying. It's the human experience.

> We grieve and grow; we hurt and hope; we get tired and keep trying.

That phrase "as we grieved, we grew" is interesting because *growth* is not usually the first thing we think of when we are mourning loss or disappointment. When we're grieving, we want relief. We want healing. We long to go back to where we were before, to the status quo. But why settle for the status quo when you could come out of this season a stronger, healthier, wiser person?

I referenced James 1 in a previous chapter. Here is a little more from that passage: "Consider it pure joy, my brothers and sisters, whenever you face trials of many kinds, because you know that the testing of your faith produces perseverance. Let perseverance finish its work so that you may be mature and complete, not lacking anything" (vv. 2–4).

"Not lacking anything" is a big promise! But that's the goal God has for you and me. Our pain isn't pointless and our suffering isn't wasted. Instead, even the difficult moments of life work for our good.

When you come out on the other side of whatever you're facing, you're going to have a list of blessings and benefits you received along the way. I'm not saying you won't have any sorrow, regret, or pain, but you'll have a lot of good things too. For the rest of your life, you'll be able to look back on this season and say, "That's where I learned [this skill, or this life lesson, or this key to success.] It was tough, and I didn't choose it, but I'm a better person because of it."

Growth Begins Within

As a kid, I remember watching my grandmother make lemonade. I don't mean the powdered Country Time Lemonade everybody buys now but *actual* country lemonade, made in the literal country, by my grandma, from scratch.

She'd start by buying a bag of lemons from the store. Before she cut and squeezed the lemons, though, she always rolled them. She would put them on the counter and press down on them with her arm, starting at her fist and ending at her elbow.

I remember asking once, "Grandma, what are you doing?"

She replied, "I'm softening the lemons."

"Why? What's the difference if you soften them or not?"

She said, "The harder I roll, the softer they get, and the more juice they give."

Here's the lesson I learned: the juice is worth the squeeze. In other words, when it comes to growth and change, the result is proportional to the pressure. The harder you get squeezed and the more challenges you go through, the more your life produces the results you want. You'll come away from that pressure with better character, greater compassion, deeper understanding, and so much more.

Too many people want lemonade without putting in the work. They want to slice open a couple of lemons, give them a few half-hearted squeezes, and then kick back on the porch with a drink in hand. That's not how it works, though. There's a lot more rolling and pushing and crushing and squeezing than that.

You might be in a rolling season right now. You might be in a squeezing season. It might feel like everywhere you turn, more is demanded of you than you can give. But keep going. The pressure is working for you. It won't last forever. Remember what the apostle Paul wrote: "For our light and momentary troubles are achieving for us an eternal glory that far outweighs them all" (2 Corinthians 4:17).

That "eternal glory" starts here on earth, by the way, and it continues into heaven. You are changed by what you go through, and that change is for the good. Your pressure will become your promotion. Your rolling will become your reward. Your squeezing will become your success. Just don't give up.

In the passage we read earlier about counting it as joy when we face trials, it's interesting that James focused on the *internal* changes that difficult times produce in us. He wrote about faith, perseverance, and maturity. When we are going through pain, our prayers are usually a lot more focused on external things. "God, I need some cash, and I need it now!" James reminds us that the real gold—the real lemonade—is the change that happens on the inside, in our character, our faith, and our walk with God.

Peter wrote something similar: "Make every effort to add to your faith goodness; and to goodness, knowledge; and to knowledge, self-control; and to self-control, perseverance; and to perseverance, godliness; and to godliness, mutual affection; and to mutual affection, love" (2 Peter 1:5–7).

Our death experiences tend to apply a lot of pressure, and that pressure often reveals cracks on the inside of us: underlying issues of the heart, soul, and mind. I'm talking about things like selfishness or greed, for example, or fear, insecurity, trauma, or bitterness. These issues and others like them might have been lurking under the surface our entire lives, but the pressure of pain suddenly makes them visible.

It's like the first rainstorm after a hot spell: Any leaks and cracks in the roof, or any windows that aren't sealed well, or any cracks along the foundation become obvious very quickly. They might have been there for a long time, but they didn't show up until the wind and rain hit full force. In the same way, when the storms of grief and loss assail us, little cracks and flaws are suddenly obvious.

That is why, once the initial grief of a loss has faded somewhat, it's good to take stock of what the pain revealed. Are you the same person under pressure as you are when things are going smoothly, or did you notice some reactions that surprised you? Have any areas of your character come to light that deserve attention? Are there issues from the past that should be addressed or people who need to be forgiven?

This is not about guilt and condemnation. I'm not saying you should beat yourself up if you didn't handle grief well. Really, does anybody handle grief well? Self-criticism is not the goal here. The goal is growth. It's to know yourself better. It's to make the most of opportunities as they arise. So when you go through hard times, let the pressure you face be a mirror that shows you more of yourself.

Remember, God promises to work all things together for your good, but the good he has in mind could include fixing up some things *inside* you. That might not be very pleasant or comfortable while it's happening, but the fruit is well worth it. When you let God deal with weaknesses, trauma, and character flaws, you set yourself up for a much stronger future.

Five Ways to Learn from Loss

What sorts of lessons can you learn in times of loss and pain? There are countless possibilities, of course, because the whole point is to know you and build you, and you are different from anyone else. However, there are some takeaways, some lessons or principles, that are common to most of our death experiences. Following are five that you will likely experience.

Learn who you are and who you can be.

At first, loss and pain feel like thieves. They take from you. They steal your joy, your opportunities, your dreams. But eventually, something interesting happens: You realize that they actually can't touch the real you. They can take away the things you *thought* were part of you, but the real you is stronger and safer than you thought, and it's also much bigger.

> You might have lost something you thought was insurmountable, but you're still here. Still standing. Still strong.

The irony of loss is that while it takes from you, it also adds to you. How? First, loss teaches you more about yourself. Going through times of pain helps you know your strengths and weaknesses, which will equip you to make smarter decisions in the future. You'll be able to trust yourself more because you'll learn where you shine, where you need to rely on others, how to leverage your strengths, and what blind spots to avoid.

Second, loss shows you what you are capable of. If you can get through tragedy, betrayal, or other seasons of deep loss, you can get through anything. You might have lost something you thought was insurmountable, but you're still here. Still standing. Still strong.

Learn to judge slowly and rarely.

Loss and pain remind you of your humanity, and that helps you have more realistic expectations of yourself and others. Rather than holding everyone to an impossible standard of perfection, you are able to show compassion, mercy, and humility.

Grief will help you release unhealthy levels of control and ego. How? By revealing in glaring detail how powerless you are to fix what is broken. That's a tough wake-up call, but ultimately it helps you become a kinder, gentler, more generous person. Kinder to others and kinder to yourself. Both are equally important.

You don't gain anything from judging everybody. That sort of approach to people damages your relationships and eats away at your own soul. You weren't built for it, and honestly you aren't good at it. Be slow to judge, slow to criticize, slow to cut people out or write them off. Like you, they are probably dealing with some pain points. And like you, they need grace.

Learn to love quickly and often.

As I mentioned earlier, your first reaction to pain and loss is probably defensive. When you're going through deep hurt, disappointment, or betrayal, you just want to survive.

That can't last forever, though. Jesus came to give you an abundant life, not a barely-keeping-your-head-above-water life. As soon as possible, open your heart to love and open your eyes to see what others are going through. Resist the urges to shut down, shut up, or shut out. You need people and people need you. Paul wrote, "Praise be to the God and Father of our Lord Jesus Christ, the Father of compassion and the God of all comfort, who comforts us in all our troubles, so that we can comfort those in any trouble with the comfort we ourselves receive from God" (2 Corinthians 1:3–4).

Comfort is something we receive and give and receive again. It's kind of like fruitcake—you always give it away, and you know that person is going to do the same thing with it. Fruitcake never dies, and neither does comfort. They just exchange hands.

Often you'll find your own healing when you help other people. There is something about reaching beyond yourself that restores the soul and heals the heart. When you give, you receive; and when you love, you are loved back.

Learn from your mistakes.

Unfortunately, people who are trying to comfort you often jump to this point way too soon. They want to tell you what you should have done or what you should do differently next time, but you're still trying to grieve.

However—and this is important—there are usually some lessons to be learned. Yes, it might be humbling to admit that you could have done something differently, but a little humility is good for everyone. And it's the first step to learning and growing, which are essential to avoid a repeat in the future.

Learn new things.

Not only will you learn from your mistakes, but you will likely find yourself branching out into new areas altogether. Loss clears space, and you get to choose how to fill that space. Again, you don't have to be in a hurry to do this. If you just broke up with your boyfriend, you don't have to fill the space he left by next week. At least not with another boyfriend. Start with a dog, maybe. They shed more than boyfriends (barely), but they aren't as needy.

Whether the loss was a person or a dream or a job or something else, it will open up room for something new. Maybe you'll discover more about yourself. Maybe you'll pick up a hobby. Maybe you'll travel to places you've never visited before. Maybe you'll restructure your priorities and discover a healthier life.

The point is to take some time to reset, rethink, and reorganize, then to move into the future. A different future than you imagined, yes—but look at the upside. It gives you space to change and room to grow.

How Have You Grown?

Think about a major loss or tragedy you experienced in the past. What did you learn? How did it change you? What doors did it open for you? How are you better because of it, and how are you worse because of it? What did it give, and what did it take? To reference Ms. Gorman, as you grieved, how did you grow? It's all too easy to remember the pain of the past, which is why it's so important to be intentional about identifying the points of change and improvement.

I'm sure you could list more than a few good things that came from that season of loss. Of course, those things don't necessarily outweigh the bad, and they certainly don't minimize it. I'm not saying growth magically makes all the pain worth it. There are some things I've suffered or lost that I don't understand to this day. I'm not sure I ever will.

Yet I have seen growth in both my character and my abilities. I've experienced new opportunities opening up for me that I wouldn't have had otherwise. I've noticed how my own pain has increased my compassion for others. While I'm sad about the losses, I'm grateful for the good that came through those losses. It's a little complicated, but that's the human experience, isn't it?

If you're currently going through a difficult season of loss and death, you don't have to have it all figured out yet. Just leave the door open for growth. When the time comes, God will show you what needs to be tweaked, fixed, removed, or added. He'll bring growth out of grief, hope out of hurt, and life out of death.

TWENTY-THREE

Dancing Pallbearers

You've probably seen the viral videos featuring what is often called the Coffin Dance. A troupe of Ghanaian pallbearers, dressed in elaborate suits and wearing sunglasses, walk down the street, balancing a coffin on their shoulders and performing impressive dance moves to loud, upbeat music. And of course, since the internet is what it is, those videos spawned countless memes and compilation videos featuring the dancing pallbearers from Ghana.

What is it about this custom that caught the world by surprise? Perhaps it's the juxtaposition of death and joy. That's the reaction I had when I first saw it. Who dances with a coffin on their shoulders? For that matter, dancing of any kind seems out of place at a funeral. Or does it? When I saw those pallbearers boldly celebrating life in the face of death, it felt *right*. It was honoring, powerful, even victorious.

According to BBC Africa, Benjamin Aidoo, the young man who started this troupe of dancing pallbearers, sees choreography as a way to honor the wishes of families who are paying their respects to a loved one.[1] Funerals are an important part of Ghanaian culture, and a funeral dance adds a unique flair to the occasion. One woman who was interviewed said this about the pallbearers: "These people, when they are taking your beloved to their final resting place, they also dance, so I decided to give my mother a dancing trip to her maker."

A "dancing trip to her maker." What an awesome way to put it! It's sad, for sure, because mourning a death is not an easy thing to walk through. But her decision to say goodbye to her loved one by organizing a dance party reveals a lot about her inner victory in the face of death.

> **Joy always laughs better, longer, and louder than death.**

It's interesting that the Coffin Dance went viral during the COVID-19 pandemic. It was almost as if we were reminding ourselves (in a weird, dark kind of way) that death doesn't get the last laugh. Joy does. Joy always laughs better, longer, and louder than death.

Joy Comes in the Morning

Even though pallbearers in our culture are generally more solemn (and less coordinated) than the Coffin Dance guys, I've still seen joy at many funerals. Actually at *most* funerals. Even in pain and sorrow, it is common to hear friends and family express joy. Often, when they get up to speak at the funeral, they laugh-cry-laugh their way through their words. When everyone meets up for the reception after the funeral, there are both tears and laughter as people remember the good times they had with the deceased.

Why is there joy? Because of the life the person led. The people they influenced. The family they raised. The friends they made. The memories they created. The love they shared. The sacrifices they made. The generosity they embodied. The legacy they left behind. The peace they now have in heaven.

David wrote in Psalm 30:5, "Weeping may stay for the night, but rejoicing comes in the morning." Paul said something similar, which I referenced in the last chapter: "For our light and momentary troubles are achieving for us an eternal glory that far outweighs them all" (2 Corinthians 4:17). Both David and Paul were able to look past the pain of the moment and see that something better was ahead.

Obviously, joy is not the first emotion you feel when death strikes. In the early aftermath of a loss, the pain is real, the hurt plunges deep, and the sorrow can feel all-consuming. Yes, weeping stays for the night—and often it's a long, dark night indeed.

All nights come to an end, though. Even the longest, darkest, saddest nights. In due time the sun comes up, the light chases the darkness away, and hope rises again. When you are weeping in the night, it's important to remember that morning is coming and joy is on its way.

Of course, you can't force joy to appear any more than you can force the sun to rise. Solomon wrote that there is "a time to weep and a time to laugh, a time to mourn and a time to dance" (Ecclesiastes 3:4). In other words, timing matters. Seasons come and go. Right now you might be weeping, and that's okay—but take heart, you won't weep forever. Today you could be mourning, but you'll be dancing soon enough. Hopefully with the same level of style as our Ghanaian brothers.

You don't need to force joy, but you should expect it. And when it comes, welcome it. Rest in it. Heal in it. Find strength in it.

Joy Gets the Last Laugh

Joy has a way of restoring your soul. There's a story in the Bible about a time of mourning that Israel was experiencing over their failures and sins. Their grief was real and it had its place, but God didn't want them to stay there forever. Nehemiah, their leader, told them, "Go and enjoy choice food and sweet drinks, and send some to those who have nothing prepared. This day is holy to our Lord. Do not grieve, for the joy of the LORD is your strength" (Nehemiah 8:10).

He wasn't shutting down their sorrow in some dismissive, toxic way. Rather, he was telling them that it was time to let their grief turn into joy. They needed to put their past mistakes and losses behind them and turn toward the future God had for them.

I love that phrase, "the joy of the LORD is your strength." Joy has a unique capacity to bring us internal strength. I don't mean fake, superficial joy but the kind of joy that comes from God. A joy that validates your weaknesses, losses, pain, or sorrow but also looks beyond them and sees the presence and power and peace of God.

Like dancing with coffins, finding joy in sorrow can seem like an odd juxtaposition. But there is power in that joy. There is freedom and triumph in being able to acknowledge death without being consumed by it.

This joy doesn't ignore your circumstances, but it does exist beyond them. That means you can be sorrowful and joyful at the same time. You can mourn your loss while still holding on to the peace and joy of the Lord. It's not one or the other but both at the same time.

Just to be clear, I'm not saying to be joyful *because* of your pain. That would be weird and masochistic. Rather, I'm saying that even in your pain, God will restore your joy. It might not happen right away and it might not take the form you expected, but I believe you will come to know God's joy on a deeper, more real level with every loss you experience.

I know I have. I can hardly put it into words, but I know what the comfort of the Lord feels like. I know what the peace of God does for my soul. I've gone through times of great loss, but God has always been faithful to give me strength and joy.

That joy doesn't necessarily feel like happiness or pleasure.

Keep that in mind. You can have this kind of joy but still not feel like telling jokes, hosting a party, or singing in the shower. It feels more like peace than happiness. It's an inner assurance that things will be okay and you will be okay. That life hasn't ended, hope isn't crushed, death didn't win.

This kind of joy is not something you can force, as mentioned earlier, but that doesn't mean it's totally out of your control. Your emotions are a product of your thoughts, and you get to choose what you think about. You can choose to be grateful, to trust, to celebrate. You can choose to look for the glimmers of light even in the darkness. After all, there are always reasons to be joyful, starting with the promise that God works all things together for good. You might have to search for a while, but eventually you'll begin to see the silver lining in the clouds.

You can't manufacture emotions, but you can choose to focus on what is good, beautiful, and hopeful. Sooner or later your emotions will catch up to your thoughts.

To be honest, I find that this is a bit of a struggle sometimes. It's all too easy to let anxieties and losses captivate your focus and fill your mind. At first you don't notice that you've lost your joy (although people around you probably do). Eventually you find yourself weighed down by the cares and concerns of daily life. That's when you have to consciously remind yourself to choose joy. God's joy is your portion. His mercies are new every morning. His love is unfailing. Think about who God is, what he's done for you, and the promises he's spoken over your future; then take charge of your reaction to pain and loss.

During the challenging transition season my family and I have been navigating lately, there have been a lot of tears, but joy has never been too far away. We've found ways to laugh, to be at peace, to enjoy life and one another and the many blessings we've been given, even though certain circumstances have been far from ideal. What other option do we have? Living under a mountain of stress or fear doesn't sound like the abundant life Jesus wants his people to enjoy. So we decided months ago that we would pursue joy, and we reaffirm that choice every day. We aren't going to wait until every problem is solved, every tear is wiped away, or every fear is conquered. Jesus is here now, and his joy is our strength.

Joy is about taking back control. It's about autonomy. When you choose joy, you refuse to let your feelings be dictated by forces outside your control. Think about that woman who said, "I decided to give my mother a dancing trip to her maker." She *decided*. She chose to incorporate joy into something that must have been emotionally hard for her. And in so doing, she got the last laugh.

Joy doesn't remove your suffering or restore your loss, of course. On the outside nothing changes. But on the inside everything changes. When your mourning begins to be transformed by the joy of the Lord, strength returns and hope arises. You gain a clearer, more positive perspective of the loss you suffered and the future that awaits.

There is triumph in that, isn't there? When you are able to find joy on the other side of grief, you are reminding yourself and the world around you that life wins out over death.

You might not be ready to dance with a coffin on your shoulder right now—literally or figuratively. That's a lot to ask. But sooner or later, the sorrow of death will give way to the joy of life. Weeping might stay for the night, but rejoicing will come in the morning.

Joy always gets the last laugh.

TWENTY-FOUR

Just Wait for It

I remember the first time I took Jen, my wife, to a Marvel movie. Once it was over, she started collecting her belongings to leave. I told her the movie wasn't over. She looked at me like I didn't know what I was talking about, because the credits were clearly rolling. Plus, some of the people around us were leaving, which only confirmed what she knew to be true: the movie had ended. I laughed and said, "Trust me, there's more to come. Just wait for it."

A few more people around us stood up, which made Jen feel more awkward and uncomfortable, especially when they had to climb over us to get out. I could tell that waiting for a mysterious something to happen seemed like a waste of time to her. After more names scrolled by than there are inhabitants in a small country, the screen faded to black. A hidden scene began: a sneak peek of another Marvel movie in the works. It was short, only a few seconds long, but the message was clear: Things were not quite as final as the movie had led us to believe. There was more to come. A sequel. Or multiple sequels, because Marvel knows how to build franchises and make money.

What's the point of these sneak peeks? They tell you the story isn't over. What looked like the grand finale in some epic battle between superheroes was not the end of their story but the end of a chapter, and there's another chapter on its way.

The same thing happens in our walk with God. Yes, we suffer loss and pain and disappointment. Those things are real, and they hurt terribly. But there is a sequel in the making. There is something to look forward to. There are still loose ends to tie up, justice to be done, characters whose stories must be written.

If you feel the credits rolling on part of your life, don't walk away too quickly. God is whispering, "Trust me, there's more to come. Just wait for it."

Maybe It's Time to Move On

The "more to come," of course, is far more valuable and exciting than yet another Spider-Man remake. It's the rest of your life. It's life after death, after loss, after pain.

That is probably equal parts exciting and terrifying. Exciting, because you know that death experiences cannot stop you, and there are good things ahead. Terrifying, because you don't know what a new normal is going to look like, and you might fear that you'll be inadequate to face whatever is next.

If you feel both of those things, I get it. I've been there. We all have. Choose to let the excitement speak louder than the fear. Loss tried to take away your power, but you can recover it by choosing to move forward. Death tried to intimidate you with its finality, but you can see farther than death because you walk by faith, not by sight.

That's a lot easier said than done, though. Especially at the beginning, when you are first processing loss. Something is over. A door is shut. A chapter has ended. A person is gone. A dream is broken. Hope is lost.

Now what? How can life continue? How can you dream again, believe again, laugh again?

Time passes, though. Maybe a few days or weeks or months. Some days are a step forward; some days are a step back. Sometimes you feel like you are totally fine, and sometimes you don't want to get out of bed. Little by little you start to breathe normally again. You look around at the pieces of your world that came crashing down, and you start picking them up.

There probably isn't one defining moment where you magically feel better, but when you look backward, you've made progress. Whether you've tried to or not, you've begun moving on.

That's what humans do after pain and loss: we figure out how to move on. We are remarkably, divinely resilient. We might not feel like it, and we definitely complain a lot along the way, but we were created with the capacity to move forward, to move past, to move up, to move on.

Now, moving on sounds impossible, even insulting, when you are first grieving. It feels like disrespect or betrayal to whatever it is we have lost. That is why if someone tells you prematurely to move on, you're tempted to bite their head off. That's the last thing you want to hear if a relationship failed, or a pet passed away, or a job didn't pan out.

But hearts heal. That's what they do. And sooner or later, even though you're still hurting, you yearn for healing and normalcy. You start whispering to yourself, cautiously and gently, *Maybe it's time to move on.*

Remember, moving on does not mean forgetting the past. If you've lost a spouse and eventually you remarry, for example, you don't erase your history with your first spouse. You used to be married to one person, and now you're married to another, and both parts of your life have validity and beauty. The same is true for any loss. You can't replace what has died, but you can turn the page and start writing a new chapter. Life is long. There are a lot of plot twists along the way. That's not a bad thing; it's a good one. Moving on from loss is a way to honor the past, not betray it, because to remain stuck in the past would waste the good things you received during that season.

> To remain stuck in the past would waste the good things you received during that season.

Moving on also does not mean you have stopped grieving. Psychiatrist Kübler-Ross wrote, "The reality is that you will grieve forever. You will not 'get over' the loss of a loved one; you will learn to live with it. You will heal, and you will rebuild yourself around the loss you have suffered. You will be whole again, but you will never be the same. Nor should you be the same, nor would you want to."[1]

Notice her emphasis not just on getting through grief but on becoming a different person: someone who is healthy and whole but who is not the same as before. If your goal in moving on is to try to get back to where you were before, you're probably going to end up frustrated. And you're selling yourself short, I might add. You are capable not just of getting through this but of being transformed, improved, and expanded in the process.

What then does moving on mean? Simply put, it means moving forward. It means making progress in the direction of whatever God has in store for you. When you build new relationships, you are moving on. When you heal emotional wounds from the past, you are moving on. When you think creatively about the future, you are moving on. When you dream and hope again, you are moving on.

There's no time frame here, no template or calendar to follow. You might run some of the time. You might walk or crawl other times. Once in a while, you'll probably be carried (or dragged) along by your friends. The point isn't how *fast* you're moving; it's that you keep moving, that you refuse to give up.

A Master Class in Moving On

The story of Ruth is a powerful example of moving forward after loss and tragedy. You might have read it before, but I'll sum it up briefly in case you haven't. There was a famine in Israel, so a married couple named Elimelek and Naomi and their two sons moved to the neighboring country of Moab to carve out a new life for themselves. Eventually, though, Elimelek died, and Naomi was left alone with her children. The two sons married Moabite wives named Ruth and Orpah. After a few years, both sons died as well. In a culture where women had few options for work, the loss of all three men would have been a crushing blow.

Naomi, discouraged and desolate, decided to return to Israel and told her daughters-in-law to stay in Moab and build lives for themselves. Orpah was fine with that, and she returned to her family. But Ruth had a different mentality. Maybe she knew her future was connected to her mother-in-law and to Israel. Or maybe she simply couldn't abandon Naomi, whom she loved deeply. Either way, she refused to remain where she was.

Ruth accompanied Naomi back to Israel, but she had no knowledge of what the future might hold. They didn't have financial support or jobs, so Ruth went out to gather leftover grain from the fields during the barley harvest. Soon she caught the eye of Boaz, the wealthy owner of one of the fields. He was impressed with her work ethic and her faithfulness to her mother-in-law, and he made sure she was safe and provided for as she worked in the fields.

It didn't take long for Naomi to realize that Boaz would make a great husband for Ruth, so she engaged in some old-fashioned match-making. She encouraged Ruth to take the initiative and approach Boaz, which she did. Boaz didn't need much convincing. Clearly he had already thought about this. Within a short time, Ruth had a home, family, love, and security.

That's the short version—the full version is found in the book of Ruth, and it's a fascinating story of Ruth's courage, love, and work ethic, surrounded by God's grace and sovereignty. It's a true story with a fairy-tale ending, but that ending only came about after a great deal of suffering, disappointment, and even death. There are several lessons we can learn from Ruth about moving forward through pain and loss.

Let love guide you.

Love guided Ruth to follow her mother-in-law to Israel, and it led her to work in the fields to provide for them. When Naomi first told Ruth that she was leaving, Ruth said these famous words: "Where you go I will go, and where you stay I will stay. Your people will be my people and your God my God. Where you die I will die, and there I will be buried. May the LORD deal with me, be it ever so severely, if even death separates you and me" (Ruth 1:16–17). She couldn't have known the end of the story, but she started by giving love—and she ended up receiving love.

When you go through loss, turn to love. If you let it guide your decisions, it will keep you moving forward.

Keep your mind and your options open.

I doubt Ruth expected to move to Israel, at least not without her husband. But when the opportunity arose, she was able to embrace it. She had the capacity and courage to imagine herself somewhere other than where she currently was, and later on she had an open mind when it came to marrying Boaz.

When you are facing a death experience, don't limit your options. Don't close your mind. Loss and pain will stir up your creativity if you let them, and the next step might be bigger and crazier and more awesome than you think.

Stay true to who you are.

Ruth was unfailingly consistent in this story. She always acted in love, integrity, courage, and humility. Boaz told her, "All the people of my town know that you are a woman of noble character" (Ruth 3:11). Whether she was changing countries, caring for Naomi, or falling in love, she made sure her actions aligned with her values.

In the same way, don't let the pain of loss lead you to act outside of who you are. Instead, be intentional about staying true to your character, integrity, and identity. Let your values anchor and ground you, and eventually your emotions will follow.

Look for the step in front of you.

Again, Ruth didn't know what was ahead. But that didn't seem to freak her out too much. She had an incredible capacity to pivot and adapt to whatever came next. For example, she knew they needed food, so she evaluated her options and took the initiative to find work. That was the next step. It ended up leading to a relationship with Boaz, and the rest was history. But Ruth didn't have all that planned out. She couldn't even have imagined it. She just knew they needed to eat, and she was strong and able to work. Since there was grain being left behind in the fields that poor people could glean, she got to work.

Like Ruth, you can't see very far into the future. Accept that ambiguity and make peace with your lack of control. Then ask yourself, *Is there a step in front of me that I should take?* If so, take it. Then look around for another step and take that. It's all you can do—and it's all you need to do.

Lean on God's sovereignty and grace.

This is the most important lesson of all. Ruth did a lot, but there's no way she could have planned or manipulated things to work out the way they did. God was in control of the story from start to finish.

God took care of Ruth and Naomi, and he'll take care of you. No matter what you're going through, you can trust that God has a master plan. He's the one writing the story, and you can rely on him to carry you through.

Mess, Mystery, Masterpiece

You probably won't find yourself gathering grain in a field, and you may or may not marry the most eligible local bachelor. Those details are unique to Ruth. But I believe your story will be just as full of God's grace. He cares about where you are. He knows what you are going through and how you are feeling. He knows where you need to go. You can trust him every step of the way. No matter what loss or pain you've experienced, God hasn't given up on your future, and neither should you.

Remember, though, that your perspective is limited to what you can see today, and you might be a long way from the future God has in mind. Don't be too quick to write things off as a total loss just because something looks like a mess. Often that mess is the early stages of a masterpiece.

My wife is an artist, and she loves to create. Halfway through the process, she'll frequently ask me what I think about her project. As I stare at an unfinished jumble of colors and lines, my first thought is usually, *What in the world is that?* I'm smart enough not to say this out loud, of course, but it must be clear on my face because she'll always ask, "Don't you like it?"

"I love it!" I'll reply as diplomatically as possible. "I'm just not sure what exactly I'm looking at."

Even when she tries explaining to me what she sees in her head, I still have difficulty visualizing it. The end product remains a mystery to me. It's not until she's finished that I see for myself what she has seen in her head the whole time. She knows what the end will be before it is complete, but I have to wait for it.

Oftentimes we can do the same thing in life. We see a mess, we see a mystery—but God sees a masterpiece in progress. Rather than judging what is happening based on the stage it is in, we need to trust the Master Artist and wait for the finished work to be revealed.

> **We need to trust the Master Artist and wait for the finished work to be revealed.**

Do things look more like a mess than a masterpiece to you right now? Are you facing a mystery, a loss, a death experience that has left you feeling confused or hurt? If so, you don't have to have everything figured out today. It will make more sense with time; but for today, you might just need to grieve, heal, and hope.

As you wait for the picture to come together, make sure you don't try to drag the past forward into the present. It's tough to move forward if you're always looking back, locked into a past you expected but never experienced. Take time to hold a figurative funeral for the things you thought you'd have by now or the things you never imagined you would lose. Identify what has died and recognize what those things meant to you. Eulogize them, remember them, honor them, mourn them.

Then bury them.

Lay them to rest. Say your goodbyes—and afterward, turn

toward life. The funeral is over now, and the world around you needs your full attention. With God's grace covering you, his love leading you, and his joy strengthening you, choose to move forward. Let God turn your endings into beginnings.

Life overcomes death, and so will you.

Part IV: Recessional

QUESTIONS FOR REFLECTION

Chapter 19. Sweet Tea and Inner Peace

1. Can you think of a time where you lost something or went through a tragedy and then found healing? Can you describe that healing process?
2. What does "acceptance" mean to you?
3. How do trust and faith in God allow you to reach a place of acceptance?

Chapter 20. Silver Linings

1. How would you define the word *gratitude*?
2. Can you be sad (or angry) and grateful at the same time? Why or why not?
3. What would gratitude look like when you're emerging from a season of loss or pain? What could you be thankful for?

Chapter 21. Between Fantasy and Certainty

1. What does the concept of hope mean to you? Why is it important?
2. What do you hope for? How do you keep that hope alive even if it takes a long time before what you are hoping for comes to pass?
3. Does your relationship with God give you hope or help you hope? In what ways?

Chapter 22. Grieving and Growing

1. How have the hard things you've gone through in life helped you grow?
2. How can you both grieve and grow at the same time?
3. What are some of the things you might be able to learn from a loss or failure?

Chapter 23. Dancing Pallbearers

1. Do you consider yourself a joyful person? How do you express joy?
2. Can joy be present during grief? What would that look like?
3. What does "the joy of the Lord" mean to you? How does he help you stay joyful when circumstances are less than ideal?

Chapter 24. Just Wait for It

1. Think about a time when you lost something important to you or went through a deep tragedy. What did moving forward or moving on look like for you?
2. What does Ruth's life story teach you about finding a positive future even after great pain?
3. What advice would you give someone who felt like they were ready to put the pain behind them and move forward? What would help them on their journey?

Notes

Chapter 4

1. *The Princess Bride*, directed by Rob Reiner (Los Angeles: Twentieth Century Fox, 1987).

2. "Old Man's Day," Parish Council Braughing, accessed January 16, 2023, https://www.braughing.org.uk/local-history/old-mans-day.

Chapter 5

1. Oscar Wilde, *The Complete Works of Oscar Wilde,* vol. 2, *De Profundis, Epistola: In Carcere Et Vinculis,* ed. Ian Small (Oxford: Oxford University Press, 2005), 85.

Chapter 8

1. James Baldwin, *Nobody Knows My Name* (New York: Vintage International, 1993), 117.

Chapter 9

1. "Fukushima Daiichi Accident," *World Nuclear Association*, Updated May 2022, https://world-nuclear.org/information-library/safety -and-security/safety-of-plants/fukushima-daiichi-accident.aspx.

2. James Brown, "I'm Shook," King Records, 1969.

Chapter 10

1. "A Conversation with Mario Andretti and Neil deGrasse Tyson," interview by Chuck Nice and Gary O'Reilly, season 4, episode 15 of *Playing with Science* podcast, July 31, 2019, Startalk, https://www .startalkradio.net/show/a-conversation-with-mario-andretti-and -neil-degrasse-tyson/.

Chapter 13

1. Brené Brown, *Dare to Lead: Brave Work. Tough Conversations. Whole Hearts* (New York: Random House, 2018), 162.
2. Propaganda (@prophiphop), "I'll say it again. Nuance is sacred work," Twitter, November 16, 2020, https://twitter.com /prophiphop/status/1328498679607558144.

Chapter 14

1. "Fastest Half Marathon Barefoot on Ice/Snow," Guiness World Records, accessed January 17, 2023, https://www .guinnessworldrecords.com/world-records/fastest -half-marathon-barefoot-on-icesnow.
2. Erik Hedegaard, "Wim Hof Says He Holds the Key to a Healthy Life—But Will Anyone Listen?," *Rolling Stone*, November 3, 2017, https://www.rollingstone.com/culture/culture-features/wim -hof-says-he-holds-the-key-to-a-healthy-life-but-will-anyone -listen-196647/.
3. Wim Hof, *The Wim Hof Method: Activate Your Full Human Potential* (Boulder, CO: Sounds True, 2020), xviii.

Chapter 16

1. C. S. Lewis, *A Grief Observed* (New York: HarperOne, 1989), 59.

Chapter 22

1. Amanda Gorman, *The Hill We Climb: An Inaugural Poem for the Country* (New York: Viking, 2021), 18.

Notes

Chapter 23

1. "Ghana's Dancing Pallbearers—BBC Africa," BBC News Africa, July 27, 2017, https://www.youtube.com/watch?v=EroOICwfD3g.

Chapter 24

1. Elisabeth Kübler-Ross and David Kessler, *On Grief and Grieving: Finding the Meaning of Grief through the Five Stages of Loss* (New York: Scribner, 2014), 230.

Acknowledgments

To my Canadian superhero, Jennifer: You have been such an inspiration and model of the message found in these pages. I know no one who exemplifies the true nature of an overcomer more than you!

To my mini-me, Maxwell Ace: When you're able to read this, know that Daddy loves you more than life itself. Let's go find some dinosaurs!

I also offer sincere thanks and gratitude:

To Alex Field and The Bindery agency: This journey has been full of twist and turns, yet full of joy. I'm so glad to be on this journey with you. There are more books to come!

To Justin Jaquith: You have been such a special gift to me and the birthing of this idea.

To Pastors Dino and DeLynn Rizzo: There is no one, and I mean no one, who loves like you both do. I owe you so much. I love you both deeply!

To my mom, Brenda Timberlake: There would be no me in ministry (or life for that matter) without you and your belief in me.

To my late father, Mack Timberlake Jr.: I miss you so much.

To Tmac and Momma MC, Kimmy, Scotty to hotty, Darrell, Nica, Dayana, Daila, Tim, Chris, Christianson, Carrigan, Quis, George, Majesty, Legend, Micah, and TT: Thank you all for loving me the way you do! And, to my knowledge, for never trying to purposely kill me!

About the Author

Tim Timberlake serves as the global senior pastor of Celebration Church, one church with seventeen locations. He is a popular thought leader, a gifted speaker, and a teacher with the ability to communicate with people from all walks of life. He also loves to use in-depth Bible teaching combined with humor to give people tools to transform their lives from the inside out. Tim is a graduate of the Pistis School of Ministry in Detroit, Michigan. He takes pleasure in the small things in life, and he is an avid sports fan. He lives in Jacksonville, Florida, with his wife, Jen, and son, Maxwell. The Timberlakes feel most alive when they are pouring back into others, and they seek to glorify God through their lives and family.